PAST LIVES REVISITED

PAST LIVES REVISITED
REMEMBERING WHO WE REALLY ARE

Healing Karmic Trauma and Karmic Grief

BOOK TWO

AURORA BOREALISZ

Copyright © 2021 Aurora Borealisz All rights reserved

ISBN: 978-1-9168734-6-9
www.auroraborealis.me

By the Author

Teachings from Amarna:
Akhenaten's Golden City
Book One

Remembering Katyn:
Memories from Beyond the Grave
Book Three

Warning

The Investigations in this Book are for information only and not for private use without adequate supervision, especially in the presence of a medical condition.

To My Mother

Contents

AD INFINITUM

Introduction

Understanding Past Lives

EVERYTHING IN LIFE has meaning. Everything that happens to us has purpose. We are not alone and help is always there for us when we need it, if we are open to receive it. I am constantly reminded of this. At the endof the 1980s, I was wondering what I should do after a cancer diagnosis, when I was suddenly inspired to attend a workshop on spiritual development. I had done this before many times, but there was an unusual urgency so I went to the workshop. I found myself talking to a woman who gave me the address of a healer who worked with crystals and with Spirit Guides. When we left, I never saw her again. I took the lead up and so began my 4-year Healing Journey with Keryaten, a Priestess of the Aten and a Friend, who lived in Amarna, Egypt, under the reign of Akhenaten, 18th Dynasty [c1353-1336BC] who came back to help me and practically saved my life, for which I will be eternally grateful to her. She told me that the purpose of this life is to clear an overload of Karmic Trauma and Karmic Grief from countless Lives as a Soldier, as this keeps me locked into an endless cycle of pain and suffering and prevents me from moving on. Images and memories of previous lives slowly began to emerge, which I recorded in a Journal, and in doing so, released and cleansed my system of trapped negative emotions and the energies attached to them and my health improved whilst doing that. Years later, I came across the extraordinary work on past life trauma and illness of Dr. Roger J Woolger, a Jungian analyst with degrees in philosophy, religion, and psychology, who successfully treated his patients with Regression *Therapy*, and was a game changer for me. I was inspired to practice on myself my own version of the *Therapy,* describing my experiences in much greater detail than before. Whilst I tried to discover who the person was, the manner of death, much depended on the last thought before dying, which would set the tone of the next life, and also whether the Soul went into the Light after Death, or remained locked behind [hauntings] where it happened, for instance, in cases of sudden, violent death amid turmoil rather than peace, as in a war situation. Often, the Soul does not know its body has died and tries to continue as if nothing had happened. But it can also be a conscious choice, or an inability to release itself from the bondage of life, because the trauma is too great. I experienced these many times. Sometimes I managed to release the Soul to the Light, sometimes not, as in the case of my life as Wilfred Owen, the Poet, whose Soul is still on the Sambre-Oise Canal where he died in 1918 aged 25 years. Many of my lives were this short, and although my average lifespan was 30-36 years, some went beyond this.

I could not control the order in which past lives came to me, their length, nor the amount of information disclosed. I simply went with the flow and recorded in my Journal everything I saw, the difficulties I experienced, the symptoms, the distress, the intensity of the emotions as I went through Death to retrieve those lives and live them again. In doing so, however, I made myself ill most of the time for years on end, as I continued the practice long-term to clear as much Karma as I could, which could never be a quick process. But I learnt a lot and released a lot, removing many obstacles in my path and greatly reducing my anxiety levels. My Spirit Guides and Helpers [family members and religious figures like Jesus, Virgin Mary, Buddha] greatly assisted me in this.

Since 2010, I uncovered over 200 past lives, and am still counting, as I am still prodding my unconscious for more. Two of these lives were from other Galaxies, from other Planets, going back in Time to some of the origins of Human Life on Earth. Many of these Lives influence me today in what I do and what I say, and I know immediately which ones they are.

I also discovered that Time does not always heal and Death is not the end of all suffering, which continues in the Afterlife and in lives to come. I am still grieving today the devastating loss of a Soulmate, and of a beloved Son, over 5000 years ago

In conclusion

This Journey has helped me understand who I really am, my weaknesses, strengths, talents, likes and dislikes, identify recurring traits fundamental to my physical and spiritual makeup which are part of my Soul essence. How people have different nationalities and roles in different lives, how foes in one life can be friends in another, and victims and tormentors can switch roles. How queens, kings, and magnates in one life can be humble and poor in another, in a never-ending cycle of karmic evolutions and learning experiences. I am amazed at what I learnt, the depth of understanding I gained of the fundamentally inexplicable mystery of Life and the Universe around us.

Farewell.

Aurora Borealisz
London 2021

Chapter 1

Extra Terrestrial

1.Another Galaxy:

A Revelation

THIS MEDITATION TOOK me by surprise.

'I recalled a Life on a Planet like Crypton in the film Superman. It was a surreal landscape, and I was standing on a rock with a man and we were both dressed in long, velvet tunics of a wonderful shade of blue and we were very, very, tall. That was a very, very long time ago.'

205. Life as An Alien:

A Big Surprise One-hour regression. Another unexpected Past Life.

'I suddenly felt and looked different. I had a small pointed face, large oblong eyes like those of a gazelle, a small pointed nose and thin mouth. I was wearing a tight black cap on my head which formed a large arch well above the eyes and narrowed down to a point between them. Also, a dress-like top, pleated horizontally with raised shoulders. I looked slim and small, although I was my actual size. I was an Alien. I came from another Galaxy, from another Planet. That was eons ago.'

Chapter 2

Ancient Egypt

11.Seti I [d1279 BC]

OUT OF NOWHERE a face appeared.

'Saw my mummy and thought it was Seti I[7]. However, I was not Seti I, but a blood relative of his.' [21.10.96]

15.A Royal Daughter [1402-1364 BC]

'I was Asipia, Eldest Daughter of Amenhotep II[23]'

16.Amarna: A Princess

'I was a Royal Daughter from Amarna and was happy there, although it was a very complex life.' [19.3.97]

32.Aisha-Ramesses II [1304-1214 BC]

'Aisha lived in Egypt-she was me-and I was beautiful and very sought after. Aisha was not Egyptian, she was half Assyrian, half Mede derivation and a very beautiful woman. I loved Egypt as my own country for my parents travelled there to live when I was tiny. There were trading and political duties for my father, and we all integrated well into Egyptian life. I always thought of myself as Egyptian for I loved my life in these times so much. My family lived at the court in Egypt and my beauty was famed. The Great King-this was the title of the King-Ramesses II[10], heard of my beauty and sought me out. He wooed me and I delighted him. He made me one of his concubines and showered me with gifts. My older life was equally happy.

I then became a minor wife. I bore my king twins and he loved both girls dearly and we all lived in comfort. I lived happily in that Life and was at peace with myself. I travelled back to the country of my birth several times. I also looked to the past and future and had vivid dreams of future events which I often told others.'

46.Flashbacks

'Valley of the Kings[23], rocks formations in the desert like mountains. I am a young man, a pharaoh. Large square, rectangular steps, large pillars, entrance to an empty space full of light. I am sitting on a throne at the other end of this space. A flow of light comes towards me. Inside this light, bamboo along the river-the Nile. Water quietly flowing; reeds/bamboo. A small basket floating on the water. Basket contains a small child-a baby. Very sweet, beautiful little baby. Sweet round face. Bit of hair, bit of blond hair. Pharaoh there bare-chested. Picks basket up. A large square. Rectangular steps. I am sitting on what looks like an elevated throne, waiting-something to arrive or happen. Images of earlier childhood: a baby, a cradle, parents looking down on the baby very loving.

A Battle

'Sitting high up looking down out on the land. There is a pass between mountains, rock formations. A battle going on, spears and arrows. They are pushed back: the enemy trying to enter the land from somewhere else. All finished'. Suddenly, an interference from another Life. 'A small girl 6 or 8-years old, dressed like an Indian girl. White feather. Indian Chief.' [10.5.13]

64.A Glimpse-The Sphinx-Khufu [c2570 BC]

'I suddenly, and unexpectedly, saw the Sphinx and

Khufu[40]. What an amazing face!' [23.7.13]

102.Ramesses II

I had a wonderful vision. The Desert lay before me in all its wild beauty and it was very hot. The colossal and powerful statue of Ramesses II shone in the brilliant sunshine in front of Abu Simbel. I went inside the temple, the inner Sanctuary, in front of three statues, two of gods and one of Ramesses in the middle. The sunlight entered this inner room bringing these statues back to life, especially the one of Ramesses and it was an incredible sight. Saw his face again, his mummy, then his statue again for a long time.' [22.5.15]

117.Looking Back

Did one-hour regression, difficult and very chaotic. Busy lines with many people waiting to come through. Started with stomach-ache, deeply seated.

Amarna - A Pharaoh

'Saw Amarna, the Golden City, gloriously resplendent in the brilliant sunshine. I was a Pharaoh, but I did not know who I was. I wore a white linen 'kilt', white linen headdress with uraeus[2], naked to the waist, sitting very erect, very athletic and very well-built.

Thebes: Khufu ['Cheops' in Greek]

Then I saw the face of another Pharaoh, in the front and by profile, Khufu[90]. Very good features.'

I moved forward in time because of an interference from 19th century South Dakota, USA.

'Saw Karnak[91], the Sacred Lake, and Sekhmet[92] for a long time in front of me.' I got palpitations and felt her strong presence. Spirit was working on my face. 'Thoth[93] also was with me for a long time, again in front and by profile, the Baboon appeared and was with me for a long time.

Hatshepsut [1507-1458 BC].

Then the Temple at Deir el-Bahri[94], Hatshepsut's Temple, went inside the inner courtyard. I was wearing the Crown of Upper Egypt and a long sleeveless tunic, and I was a Pharaoh [man or woman?]. Beautiful. He/she was by profile with the Crown of Upper and Lower Egypt and also Hatshepsut[95]' Again, I felt the deeply-seated pain in my solar plexus and did not know why. I tried to release it by taking it up to the Light and felt something moving from my stomach up through the mouth and out. A release. Was she murdered? [10.6.15]

147.Pre-Dynastic Egypt-Before 5000 BC

'I am in the Desert, the wind blows the sand, a sand storm is approaching like a huge wave of dust sweeping across the Desert, engulfing all it encounters, a white dense mass devouring everything that stands in its way, frightening, the sky disappears, threatening. I am tall, young and good looking, black liquid eyes, wear a turban and a white tunic, my skin is dark. I stare into the Desert, the sand is golden, the sky is deep blue and all is peace-a caravan of people and camels carrying goods pass me by, there is an oasis with water and palm trees.

I am a much older man now, still with a white turban and tunic, sandals. I have a thick, white, moustache, feel sadness in my heart. The people from the east [I see the Desert, but I am actually looking west] came on us like locusts, hungry and angry. They took our harvests and possessions, and stole our women. We violently clashed with them, with ferocity, many of us died, the desert sand red with blood. We fought and fought them until we pushed them back, pursuing them back into their lands.

I see a mud-brick village resplendent in the strong sunlight. We all joined in the fight- young and old- I lost two sons. Will they come again?

I am a strong man, but I cry. I dug a deep hole in the desert sand and placed the bodies of my two sons in it and bade them goodbye. Ah, the pain of it all! I watched them disappear as I threw the sand into the pit until it was full and there was no trace of it.

That was some time ago, but the pain is still there, their memories alive in me. I am an old man now and look back to the past as I have no future. My wife died years ago, and I am alone. We have been at peace since we last fought the Easterners, we beat them so badly, they dared not come back. Our village is thriving, the harvests are good, the Nile plentiful.

I spend my days sitting on the riverbank crying, thinking about my sons, and the pain does not go away. I will soon join them and we shall be together again. I am very old. Villagers find me there, carry me home and lay me on the floor, they will bury me in the desert, with some possessions. It is over.' What was the last thought? There is a spasm in my solar plexus, rising into my heart. 'I felt regret that my sons died before me, young, they never had a life of their own. I called them out as I gently stepped out of my body. Death was kind to me. I was eager to go and floated up towards a big round Light shrouded in a misty halo, like bright moonlight in the dark-blue sky.' I cry. [13.1.16]

Chapter 3

Tutankhamun [r.1347-1337 BC] Ankhesenamun

3.The Royal Palace Amarna[73]

'THERE IS A very beautiful, young Egyptian woman inside a palace with a walled garden and a pool in the garden with flowers, a very private garden [Amarna, the Golden City]. She is in the garden now, near the pond, very peaceful setting, the interior of an Egyptian Palace, very peaceful and beautiful, very clean. Lotus flowers in the water, very peaceful setting, daytime, early afternoon, the sun is very strong and very hot, but it is lovely, it is a quiet moment. I look into the water, it is very still, very clear. As I look into the water, I feel its coolness, refreshing, a very powerful feeling as I feel the water, I touch the water with my hand and the lotus flower opens. I see a reflection of my face in the water as I look down and the water is around me. I am kneeling on the edge of the pool looking into the water and going into the water, but I am not afraid. I am in the water now and I am under water, but I can breathe. It is a very refreshing and soothing experience-it is a big pool. The water is very clean, very healing, it covers me entirely.

At the edges of the pool there is someone. I am Egyptian. I am dressed in white, my hair in the Egyptian style. I am moving in the water and enjoy walking in the water, moving around and doing pirouettes. It is very healing, and the lotus flowers are on the surface of the water.

I am coming up to the surface, stepping out of the pool,

there are these people holding towels and wrapping them gently around me to dry me and change my clothes and I feel and look refreshed and renewed. A beautiful headdress with a golden snake in the middle is put on my head and my hair is straight and combed and neat and I now sit on a stool at the edge of the pool. They seem to be fussing around me, adjusting my clothes, making me look very regal. I feel rejuvenated after this wonderful bath into this wonderful pool with lots of flowers. I sit there quietly on this beautiful lacquered stool, enjoying the peace of the moment. A small, round, black onyx cup is brought to me with some liquid, water, pure water. I drink it and feel refreshed as if a new life is coming to me.

The girls are waiting on me, kneeling around me, some wave their fans a little to give me a bit of coolness. It is a very hot afternoon, they brought me refreshment, I sit quietly enjoying the peace of the garden. It is a very special moment.

There is a man, dressed royally with a short kilt, folded in the front, naked to the waist, wearing a crown with a snake in the middle [uraeus] and jewels on his chest. He just appeared from the Palace and is walking towards me. All the young girls giggle with excitement and disappear as he comes towards me and we are left alone as I stand and he comes towards me and embraces me, embraces me. It is a beautiful moment, beautiful moment, beautiful moment. I am in his arms and we just stand quietly, without moving, his arms around me. I am still, peaceful and happy. It is a long moment of happiness, a long embrace.

The scene is different. People dressed with heavy gowns, and tall headdresses made of gold, they are moving in a procession towards a Temple, these people dressed in white, their tall headdresses made of gold, in front, leading the way, all dressed in white. There are two sedan chairs carried by priests dressed in white, their heads shaven. In one there is a woman dressed in white, with dark hair, in the other chair the Pharaoh with a beautiful headdress, naked to the waist, wearing a white short gown folded in the front and jewels on his chest. We are carried side by side by all these priests dressed in white, their heads shaven, the priests at the front of this procession with their tall, gold headdresses. They move slowly, slowly, towards the Temple, between two rows of priests, all white. Priests simply dressed in white with no ornaments, their heads shaven. As the procession reaches the entrance of the Temple, more priests come out to meet us. The sedan chairs are lowered gently to the floor so that the two people can step down, they join together, hand in hand, and walk up a few steps towards the priest with the heavy jewelled gold headdress who is waiting for them. They all move towards the entrance of the Temple and go hand in hand and disappear into the Temple. They go inside the Temple into a huge room, huge, huge room, filled with priests wearing large gold headdresses and chest jewels, vast amounts of glittering gold. They all talk very loudly and excitedly, the buzzing noise is deafening, but it all suddenly stops as the royal couple appear and reach the other side of the room.

A Coronation

They go up a few steps and there are two thrones on top of the steps and they sit on the thrones together and all the priests, all the priests in this huge room chant, they all chant and their voices sound excited and happy, they sound excited and happy. I see the Pharaoh's face and his wife sitting next to him on the throne. He is being given Golden Staffs by the Chief Priest which he now holds with his hands crossed on his chest, and he is standing holding them on his chest, and his wife raises to her feet and stands close to him. They come down the stairs now and walk amongst the priests and go out to the front of the Temple to salute the people waiting down the steps, at the bottom of the Temple, waiting for them to appear. As they appear from the entrance of the Temple, they greet their people and all the priests that are waiting and all the crowds, there is a huge roaring cheer, deafening, like an explosion, a feeling of festivity and happiness in the crowds under the sun, but the scene is moving further and further away. I see the royal couple waiving their hands to the people, but I hardly see them as I am fast travelling back in Time. Suddenly, there is a Nun, a

Catholic Nun, in front of me like a station marker, coming down to more recent times, but I can still see this picture of jubilation in this Temple behind this Nun, the sunshine, gloriously bathing everyone'.

7.Karnak Temple[91]

Pharaoh clothed in gold, with a beautiful face, the face of a young boy, short black hair, with black fringe, beautiful large black eyes, lovely little nose, lovely little mouth, lovely little face, 7/8 years old, and in the background, the Pharaoh's face, the boy's face and a Temple with columns. Again, the Pharaoh, with a beautiful headdress with the snake and the hawk, is holding the hand of the child, the same child, standing at the entrance of the Temple with his back to the Temple, looking ahead of him in a large square. A god, half human, with the head of a hawk[24], [Horus] is holding this child, the hand of this child, and he too has his back to the Temple, the child seems to be a boy, but it could be a girl. The God with the face of a hawk, a large beak for nose, the head of a bird; my own face, my mouth is getting larger and thinner, my nose, what is a nose feels like a beak; my eyes are very squashed, they are going inwards deep down; I feel as if I have the face of a hawk myself. I see the head of a hawk by profile.

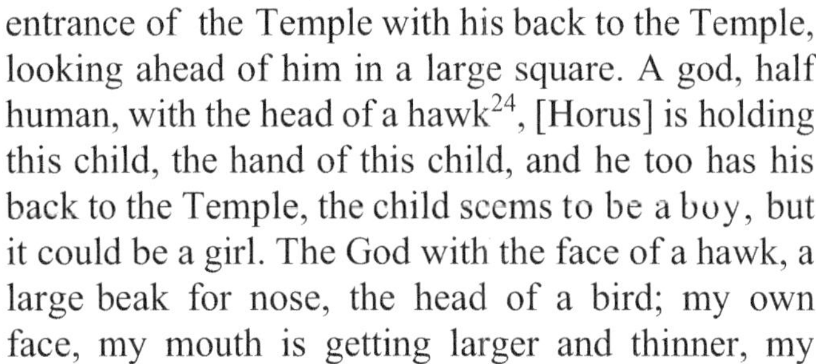

Ankhesenamun

I am a High Priestess and wear a hawk mask during ceremonies and take up the qualities of the Hawk. I can see the head of a hawk by profile–a dark entrance behind him. This God is in front of me, with the face of a hawk [Horus], a kind of long hair on his head. Again, this huge white Temple and steps leading up to it, the sky is blue, a lovely day, the sun is shining. I see Horus by profile and also in the front; he is holding the hand of a small child [4/5 years old] with long hair, a lovely face the little child, the Temple behind hm. The Pharaoh superimposed on this picture, his face. The Temple is beautiful, colossal, very impressive. The entrance to the Temple between the columns is very dark even if outside the sun is shining very brightly. [Karnak Temple]'

I see the face of a young man, adolescent, short hair, good features, the Temple behind him. The Pharaoh dressed in light clothes as usual. I see the inside of a walled garden with a pool in the middle and a Princess with short hair and a lovely jewel on top of her hair, she is wearing a beautiful white dress, looks like the woman in the paintings of Tutankhamun [Ankhesenamun] looks like a painting herself, not a real person, she looks like that picture of Tutankhamun with her giving him some refreshment. Yes, it is the painting of Tutankhamun sitting, his wife giving him some refreshment, a fresco on a wall somewhere in a tomb.

A Tomb in the Desert[25]

Out into the sunshine, into the desert, this woman with white hair wearing a cloak, a fat fellow with a bald head [a priest] wearing a tunic, there seems to be a 'passage' going down, with steps going down, the sun is shining, it is a beautiful day outside, there is a High Priest with a big golden Crown, it must be a Pharaoh, a high golden Crown like a triangle but curved at the top with a snake in the middle, an unusual Crown. There is an entrance with stones around it, the entrance is going down, there is a Roman General [a Spiritual Guide], the entrance looks like a well; a good-looking Roman with a mantle, standing at the entrance of this, whatever it is–looks like a tomb. He has taken an Egyptian woman by the hand, and they are walking through the passage, he has a very good face, very good looking, they have come out into the light somehow, they are out into the open and the light is shining on them. [The Valley of the Kings]' [11.8.94]

22.A Tragic Death

'In that life, Tutankhamun was murdered, after being weakened by poison. His death was long and drawn out. The poison weakened him and caused an illness which inhibited his travelling around. The end was brought on by a fall from a chariot– the wheel was not put on properly and it came off when travelling at high speed, causing him to fall and hit the back of his head on a rock. The last image he saw was that of a falcon soaring up into the sky: he became the falcon and his soul left the body.

A Strong Ruler

Tutankhamun put a lot into this life. He was not a weakling boy-king subservient to a mentor. He was a strong ruler, an adult man in a young man's body and knew his role and his duties in life. He knew what he was doing and what he wanted to achieve. He wished to make major changes in people's consciousness. It worked for a while, but people slipped back and power, influence, and intrigue, became once more the norm of the royal court.

Smenkhare [r. 1351-1348 BC]

Tutankhamun wanted to go back to more gods, but also improve the changes made by Akhenaten. Between their reigns, there was the brief one of Smenkhare[17] which caused enormous problems, because he was much more extreme, with no real vision or foresight and made many mistakes in judging the characters of high officials.

Mission Impossible- King Ay [r.1337-1333 BC]

Tutankhamun's aims were to improve the political system, reduce corruption, reinstate the Old Gods, but keep the purity of worship and regime which Akhenaten had envisioned. This involved changing officials and power structure and was not popular and created many enemies. He was succeeded by Ay[77]- an old friend who had been with Akhenaten, but Ay was not his murderer. Ay was in fear for his own life. Ay was like a father to Tutankhamun, who had very little fatherly support in his early years. He died young, but his soul was advanced. He started the spiritual work and understanding of the necessary changes by the time he was seven years old.

A Third Marriage

After Tutankhamun's death, as Ankhesenamun I faced a difficult time, but my position enabled me to continue a luxurious life. Great emotional distress, pain and anguish resulted from this loss. Anyway, I managed. I missed him, but life went on. I married a man I did not love-a wise and diplomatic move. He did not really bother me and took care of me in his own way, but I was not his love and he was not mine. My marriage took me out of a vulnerable position where I too could have been murdered and, for that reason, it was necessary.' [16.6.98]

40.A Young Boy

'I felt a great oppression and pain in the heart chakra as I quickly went back to a Life in Egypt and discovered beautiful, but very painful memories.

'Saw Tutankhamun[17] as a beautiful little boy with his little crown, and as a 13/15-year-old teenager, always with his crown.' [15.3.2009]

63.Flashbacks

'For the first time ever, I saw Tutankhamun's real face extensively and not as a mortuary mask as I normally do, but as a beautiful little boy with his crown. I also caught a glimpse of Akhenaten. Then a man in modern clothes appeared, dressed in deep blue with a tinge of red in it, blue shirt, open necked, rolled up sleeves, possibly 60 years old, bald on top, head like a dome, with a crown of wispy white hair. My Mother also appeared and a young pharaoh with a white crown and white loin garment-it was me'. I felt a very strong pain in my solar plexus. 'I see Tutankhamun again as a 7/8-year-old boy with a crown, I see his beautiful face'. [22.7.13]

74.Visions

'Regressed to Ancient Egypt and saw Tutankhamun. Caught a glimpse of Ankhesenamun as she really was: a young, very beautiful woman with a small, delicate face.' Their minimalist portraits which have come down to us are very accurate. [4.8.13]

79.Tutankhamun's Death

'After trying a few times these days without success, I had a breakthrough. I was able to go into Tutankhamun's death and feel his pain for the first time, though not in full, it would be too strong, but a beginning of it, something I was not allowed to do in the past. I saw him with Ankhesenamun, and as a boy, sweet and beautiful, and caught a very short glimpse of the scene of his death, in his bedchamber and on his bed, not dead yet.'

88.Memories of a Distant Past

A two hours long regression. 'I went back to Egypt and the Valley of the Queens[58], to Hatshepsut's tomb[59] then to the Valley of the Kings, to Tutankhamun's tomb, and memories flooded in. The goddess Sekhmet appeared, I felt her presence, but lost the link. Also, the god Osiris was with me for some time. Saw Ankhesenamun briefly as she was in real life, young and beautiful, and felt the pain of her death, but could not get details of her last thought'. [12.9.13]

113.Thebes: A Funeral

'I was an Egyptian princess, wearing a tight dress and a wig with uraeus. Saw Amarna spread out under the brilliant Sun, beautiful city, its large Central Avenue. Saw young Tutankhamun[83] like a painting [mortuary mask], large beautiful eyes and face. Saw the Valley of the Kings[84] sun-baked in the midday sun, intense blue sky and the golden sand. I saw a small procession of two or three people following a body, a funeral, entering a tomb and going down. Oh, how my heart aches!

An Uncertain Future

I am sitting in a corner of a rectangular room[85] in the torch light, lost in thoughts. What will the future hold? I am beautiful, with a little face and large intelligent eyes, black hair cut in the Nubian style.'

I felt an overwhelming pain in the solar plexus [stomach] right up under the top ribs. I asked Ankhesenamun[86] what happened to her when Ay died, Horemheb[87] did not marry her, the last true royal blood. Could not get anywhere, it was a very complex life. [3.6.15]

117.Thebes: A Desert Funeral

I saw the golden mask of Tutankhamun, the funeral procession in the Desert to his tomb, with two or three people dressed in black, against the white-golden sand resplendent in the blazing sunshine [early morning].'

155.Amarna: A Short Visit

'During a short meditation, I fell into a slumber and found myself back in Amarna, resplendent in the sunlight. Vast city of low, mudbrick constructions in the desert.

I saw Ankhesenamun as a young, slim, beautiful woman with a small face and large, soft, sensitive, intelligent eyes, a small round mouth; short black glossy hair with a long fringe Nubian style. Exactly as she appears in those minimalist Egyptian murals.' [26.9.16]

170. Riding in the Desert

Suddenly, I see rock formations, the Valley of the Kings, Tutankhamun wearing a white tunic and gold round crown on a horse, about 14 years old, tall, manly. He looks very much like his portraits/statuettes, very beautiful face and large, soft, intelligent eyes.' [22.8.17]

187.A Loving Family

Immediately I woke up, I felt very tense and knew there were emerging Memories and decided to investigate. This is a difficult Life to retrieve. There is a lot of resistance, a big trauma. My agitation makes it more difficult to access this Life. I feel pain rising from the solar plexus. My Mother and my Grandfather are here to assist me. At last, something very vague is beginning to appear in front of me. It is very hard, like extracting a tooth with very deep roots.

'A Catholic Nun with roses appears [Saint Rita da Cascia[71]]. It has been a long time since She last visited me and I am very happy to see Her. I begin to relax and sink into myself'. I see the Desert and the Pyramids in the distance. It is a very hot day and a light haze in the sky makes it look like dreamland. Akhenaten is next to me, his face close to mine. He has beautiful, liquid,black eyes. Amarna is glittering in the sunshine. I see palm trees, the central avenue. What a glorious city! A jewel, resplendent in the Desert.

I see Ankhesenamun for the first time. I was never allowed this before. She is very slim and beautiful, small face, nose, and mouth, large, intelligent eyes. Her hair is short, in the Nubian style. Her memories of this time are happy ones, and so are those of Tutankhamun. As children, they enjoyed the love of their parents in a very closely knitted family circle, but there were deaths, too. That was some-time ago.

King Tutankhamun-A World of Deceit

Ankhesenamun is walking through the high columns of Karnak. They are back in Thebes, now. Their parents are dead, and Tutankhamun is King now. Although young, he is a strong, innovative force and this has created enemies in a strong, conservative base, as he pushes ahead with his reforms. They are in the Throne Room, a vast enclosure full of Courtiers, Priests, top Army men, a very beautiful couple, very much in love, Soul Mates. He is very tall and slender, athletic like his Father, with a very beautiful and intelligent face. Ankhesenamun is smaller, but equally beautiful. They are very vulnerable, surrounded by strong enemies. Although the King holds the power, that power can be taken from him. He is no longer a God on earth, remote and unassailable, but a man like any other. Akhenaten died a natural death. He died of the Plague, as did Nefertiti. Tutankhamun was murdered.' [17.1.18]

188.Karnak

'I see very tall columns, Karnak Temple in Thebes, Ankhesenamun walking between them. I see her very clearly, as never before. I was not allowed this, too much trauma. I wish I could draw her face well. She is very beautiful, exactly like her paintings with Tutankhamun: a good minimalist portrait of them both. I see the Sacred Lake [Karnak] early morning, Then, Ankhesenamun again, her little, wonderful face and sensitive eyes with a life of their own, exquisitely beautiful and delicate in appearance.

A Man with a Lion's Courage

I am Ankhesenamun. I am sitting at my desk writing this. Tutankhamun knew how strong the opposition to his reforms was. He knew he was in danger, but decided to push them through. Perhaps he should not have, perhaps this would have saved his life, but he was not to compromise on what he thought was right and essential. He was a young, but strong, determined man, muchmore mature than his young years. He was not afraid. He had led his men in battle with his generals. He was a brave man, with a lion's courage. He was not afraid of anything.

A Murder Plot

Bribery and corruption infiltrated his inner circle and those who were meant to protect him, his bodyguards. It was meant to look like an accident. One of the wheels of his chariot was loose and came off while he was riding in the desert causing him to fall and hit his head on a rock, losing consciousness. He was taken to the Palace and laid on his bed, his physicians around him, anxiously examining him. With no obvious signs of injury, they feared the worst. They could not deal with an internal injury. It was some time before Tutankhamun regained consciousness. He was in great pain. I assisted him and saw him slowly decline. It was terrible to see. He got weaker and weaker every day, could hardly eat, was in very great pain during short periods of lucidity, talking very little. I stood by his side day and night. I was traumatised seeing his life slowly ebb away, unable to do anything. I felt in danger. I could breathe danger in the air around me, I could 'touch' it, so palpable it was. I suspected every single one of our attendants. It was terrible.

A Slow Painful Death

It was terrible to witness this decline. Tutankhamun, in the flower of his youth, delirious, feverish, in very great distress, his bedclothes drenched with his sweat. I awaited the inevitable with dread, fearing for my life and for what the future would bring.

Tutankhamun lingered on a week or two, perhaps a bit longer-I cannot remember. My life had fallen apart. I lost the man I loved, my Soulmate. I was now alone and in danger myself. Everything seemed to collapse. There was nothing there for me. Losing Tutankhamun was the greatest misfortune of my life then, and forever, through Eternity. His funeral was quick. It was the height of Summer and it was very hot. The body could not be kept for long.

A Desert Funeral

It took place early one morning, a small procession of two, three people in all. Ay was there, supporting me. He too, was shattered. He loved Tutankhamun like a son, and loved me too. With Tutankhamun's death my Dreams died and were buried with him and I faced the emptiness of a whole life without him.'

I am astonished at the Reality of this Truth. Never in my life I was granted knowledge of the Events that led to his death: it would have destroyed me. Now I can take it. Who were his assassins?

'Strangely enough, Horemheb was not one of them, though he greatly benefited from Tutankhamun's death. The conspirators were the top aristocracy, including priests, those hit most by Tutankhamun's reforms.' Perhaps it will be revealed to me who they were, but one fact remains: Tutankhamun lives on through millennia and is now world famous, more than a rock star. He has truly achieved Immortality, while they have decayed and disappeared into nothingness, nobody remembers them, they are truly dead. This, in a way, is his revenge. They are truly dead, lost forever, nobody knows who they were, nobody remembers them, and this may be the reason why their names are concealed from me. I am overwhelmed by a wave of great anger and have to stop. [18.1.18]

189.Life Without Tutankhamun

I still feel agitated and uneasy. There is a lot to discover. I am overwhelmed by the amount of information I now receive. For most of my life I have tried hard to go back and have been firmly frustrated by Spirit in my attempts. I could not have withstood the memory of what happened then: it would have been fatal to me. Even now, there is a Veil of protection around me which lessens the emotional impact of these revelations as they come to me. I get all sort of images, confusing, they come in all together.

Another Murder-Married to Ay-Death of Ay

'After the burial, we returned to the Palace, a dismal and dangerous place for me. I knew I had to act fast, to save my life. I could not dwell on my sorrow. I needed someone to protect me. I needed a husband. I wrote letters to one of our Allies who had many sons and offered to marry one and make him king of Egypt. I can imagine his surprise at this unusual step, and I too was surprised at myself. He agreed to my request, but his son never made it to Egypt. He was murdered on the way. I felt very sorry for him. I had underestimated the speed and the amount of information available to my enemies. I am very angry, even now. It was someone very close to me who supplied this information, perhaps a lady in waiting. I had many. I had not been careful enough to conceal my plan. I was terrified. I felt surrounded by spies, but I behaved with composure and kept my nerve. This saved my life, as it reassured my enemies and it was to save me again a few millennia later, in another Life in England. I was sure they were quite a few disgruntled courtiers and priests wanting to keep their status and wealth. Horemheb was policing the Empire far away and could not help me there and then. I had to act quickly. I married Ay, who was like a father to me, and the situation normalised. But Ay[77] was old and died. I was left alone again and unprotected.' [19.1.18]

190.An Uncertain Future

Today I feel extremely low and very fearful-of what, I do not know. This is not my fear, it is Ankhesenamun's fear, my depression is her depression at Tutankhamun's death, the precariousness of her situation and the uncertainty of her future. It is so strong that it is almost unbearable. It is a blind fear, unmitigated fear which strikes out suddenly, prevents me from living my life, and against which there is no protcction. The loss of Tutankhamun is a major source of sorrow and disquiet which combined with the existential fear she is experiencing, is deadly. I wonder how she survived its impact. A weaker person would have been crushed by its weight. Not Ankhesenamun, who was made of steel under a coat of velvet. Suddenly, a very beautiful Fox appears, her face very close to mine, staring into my eyes. She is very beautiful.

Thanksgiving for All that is Beautiful in Life

'I see a passage between very tall columns [Karnak Temple], priests dressed in white. I am dressed in white. I see Anubis, the God of the Dead and my Protector. I see vegetation and wildlife. I see the Life-giving Force, the Nile. I see crocodiles resting on the riverbanks, birds flying. It is heaven on earth. I praise Amun-Ra for all this wealth, for all this beauty. I praise the Gods that give us Life and make us strong and powerful.

The Throne Room

A vast Throne Room is filled with white-robed High Dignitaries and Priests, covered in gold, solid gold, their necklaces and headdresses reflecting the light pouring from the ceiling, making one dizzy with so much gold. They talk with great animation and the sound of their voices is deafening.

How many traitors among them, ready to strike?

They hold powerful posts throughout the E m p i r e . They have their own armies. Their loyalty depends on the favours [tax exemptions, and so on] and wealth they make from service to the Crown. The King has a very powerful, loyal, Army. It keeps the Empire together and silences the opposition.

I see hippos on the riverbanks and in the water, happy and relaxed. Life is rich, full of the Gods' blessings.

For how long?

I see Horemheb[75], a tall, imposing, authoritative man with an impenetrable face made of granite, seldom smiling. Impossible to gauge his thoughts, he would be a deadly adversary with total control of the Army. Fortunately for Us, he is on Our side.' I feel a lot of pain raising from the solar plexus, rushing up with force.

King Horemheb [1333-1305 BC]

'We were happy, fulfilled in each other's company. We were Soulmates. We wanted a family, a happy family like Our Parents. All that was taken away from Us by a few corrupt and disaffected officials and priests. They did not enjoy the fruits of their treachery for long.

When Ay died, Horemheb[87] succeeded him. He ruled the Empire with steely, ruthless, determination. Everybody was brought down to their knees to obey him. It worked, but did not bring Tutankhamun back and did not restore Our lives they had destroyed.

Married to Ay [r. 1337-1333 BC]

My marriage to Ay, and the backing of Horemheb, took me out of danger. When Ay died a few years later[77], Horemheb succeeded him, although not of royal blood. I was the last true Royal Blood Princess. Blood Royalty died with me. Why did I not marry Horemheb?

He did not need to marry me to justify his elevation to Royal. He seized the Throne as a matter of fact. I could not prevent this, nor was I prepared to risk my life again, trying to stop him. He had the support of the Army, I was only a woman, though pure Royalty, and had no troops to support me. Horemheb allowed me to maintain a rich, comfortable lifestyle. I kept my high status as a Royal Princess, but had no authority. I preferred it this way. I was safe, as I was no danger to anybody and it wasbetter to have Horemheb on my side than against me. I did not have to marry again, but I did.

Another Wedding

I married a man of non- royal blood of very great wealth and spent my life in great comfort, always remembering my true Love, Tutankhamun. I often felt his presence and this reassured and comforted me, gave me strength to face another day, another year. In this way, it was a lonely life. I did not love my husband and he did not love me. But we managed. He was older than me, though not as old as Ay, in his forties.' [23.1.18]

191.The Last Day

Ankhesenamun appears, young and beautiful. There is a lot to clear in that Life and it is all surfacing. Now is the time. My Mother and Grandfather are here to protect me.

'I see a rectangular garden, surrounded by columns, and a rectangular pool in the middle with fish in it and flowers in the water and in the garden. It is early morning and I walk in the garden, amongst the flowers. I am happy. Tutankhamun joins me and embraces me. There is such a feeling of fulfilment in that embrace, two Souls joined together. And yet, all that happiness was to be taken away from Us!' I am overcome with a deep feeling of uneasiness. Something is stirring in my solar plexus.

'It is a cool morning. The start of a beautiful Day and

Tutankhamun is riding his Chariot in the Desert, followed by two Bodyguards. He is happy. He is wearing a small, rounded Crown, chest jewels, naked to the waist, short white kilt and sandals. He is tall and athletic and breathtakingly beautiful. He regularly rides in the Desert early in the morning, before it gets too hot. But today it will be different. It will be his last. He is riding at great speed with two horses for extra power. He is a very skilled horseman. One of the wheels is loose and suddenly comes off, causing the Chariot to sway throwing him off, hitting his head against a stone, while the horses continue to run, but they are quickly brought under control by the bodyguards. He is unconscious and is taken to the Palace, where his physicians gather around him. There is nothing they can do.

A Slow and Painful Death

Oh, the shock and horror of that moment when I saw Tutankhamun lifeless in his couch! I thought he was dead, but he lingered on, a very slow, very painful death. I spent my whole time with him and witnessed the horror of it all, forever imprinted in my Soul. I banished all attendants and nursed him myself. I was told what happened and knew it was not an accident. I did not want to see anyone. I trusted no-one. I feared the informer was still with us.

Both Ay and Horemheb rushed to the Palace to follow developments, and a state of emergency was imposed on the Empire, security was tightened, but it was too late. Tutankhamun died and most of myself died with him. The bewilderment of what followed was too much for me to bear, but bear it I did. The rushed embalmment, funeral, the Palace rooms once full of joy and now empty, my life devoid of meaning. Danger all around me.

Ay and Horemheb kept close watch over me; they were always with me and we discussed what to do. I made my own decisions, but listened to their advice, I felt I could trust them. I had no-one else to listen to, certainly not the High Priests and Courtiers! I did what I could in the circumstances, but it misfired and a young, innocent man died as a result. I was devastated when I was told of his death.' [24.1.18]

209.Memories

Recently, my anxiety levels increased, and I decided to discover the cause of this.

'I am slowly sinking into a past Life, going through layers of pain and discomfort, but no images yet. I go through a long, narrow passage between a long row of tall columns [Karnak]. The sun is high in the sky. I am back in the Valley of the Kings. I see Tutankhamun and feel the pain of his death, the emptiness, the prospect of a life without him. It is devastating. Recently, he came to me several times, I miss him more than ever, nothing has changed. I see Hatshepsut's Mortuary Temple. I am greatly distressed. I look for answers and find none.' [6.7.21]

210.A Pain that Never Dies

I woke up at about 3 am at the start of a panic attack, which fortunately did not happen. I had this at regular intervals in the last seven months, or more, as there is a Past Life trying to emerge into consciousness. I was unable to follow this up until now. Memories are stored in my left leg. I relax the muscle and breathe up from the left foot to the crown chakra, to release them.

'The funerary coffin of Tutankhamun appears. He is very beautiful.' There is a lot of pain in the heart chakra, and I do not know if I can access it, whose pain was it, anyway? My Mother appears and I ask for her help, feel tired and want to close. There is a lot of Sorrow in the heart chakra and I would like to retrieve and clear it. There is a strong pull upwards and outwards, but cannot release it yet.

'Tutankhamun is here.'

I ask for help, and walk through a long corridor between very high columns [Karnak Temple?]. Lots of throat clearing, heart chakra sore. I focus on my left foot and start rocking to and fro in my chair. I repeat the process through the right leg, as something strong is moving upwards to the heart chakra, through my throat, perhaps something is leaving. It might have done so, as I feel a lot lighter, and much better. [13.11.21]

Chapter 4

Akhenaten [r. 1353-1336 BC]-Nefertiti

88.Two Beautiful People

'NEFERTITI CAME IN and was with me a long time. I first saw her head as she was, a beautiful woman. Then I saw her full figure with her 'round' crown, wearing a long, white cotton dress, no jewellery, truly breath-taking! Akhenaten appeared briefly as he was in life, very good- looking, and Tutankhamun as a boy, but more like a portrait, not yet the real person'. [20.8.13]

104.Visions of Egypt

'Saw a tall man, black short hair, wearing a tunic under a red mantle, sandals, young [30ish] good-looking; the Valley of the Queens, Hatshepsut's temple; Amarna, the Throne room, Akhenate**n** dressed in white, with white head covering [not a crown] saw him really well for a long time, sitting, he became me, but I do not think I was him in that life, he was my Father. Saw Tutankhamun as a boy, what a beautiful little face! Large, intelligenteyes, how lovely!' I could not go further into that life, but Akhenaten was with me for a long time. A great wave of sadness came over me and I could not shake it off. [24.5.15]

105.Akhetaten: A Desert Flower

I caught a glimpse of Nefertiti, the Desert, and the beautiful town of Akhetaten[73] baking under the hot sun, the large central avenues, and Akhenaten driving a chariot, also the Throne room, a very large pillared hall with sunlight pouring on the throne from an open ceiling at its further end.

A Beautiful Man

I saw Akhenaten[74] good-looking and perfectly formed, features like those of his statues, but smaller and regular. Saw courtyards, trees, plants and flowers. Amazing! Kept seeing the Throne room and Akhenaten wearing the tall crown and also the white wig and the typical Egyptian 'kilt'.' Could not get how he died, was it murder, illness, or what? 'Saw the goddess Sekhmet a few times, and felt something on my face and throat. The Desert was beautiful, very blue sky and very hot. What an amazing sight!' [23.5.15]

Horemheb Speaks: The Truth

Suddenly, Horemheb[75]appeared out of the blue, a bit dim at first, then very clearly. I asked him if he wanted to speak through me, which he did with a deep authoritative voice, especially when he said: 'I have spoken' three times, a very powerful, very dangerous man.

Horemheb's speech:

'I served under Amenothep III and was loyal to him.
I served under Amenothep IV and I was loyal to him.
I served them well.'

Rebellion-Famine-Plague-Death of Nefertiti

There was a rebellion in Nubia and I went there to restore order. Went to Thebes, people were angry because of bad harvest, granaries were low. People thought the gods were angry because they had been neglected. Nefertiti went to Thebes to place offerings to Amun and calm the people who were starving. Then illness struck the weakened people and many died, including warriors and officials. Nefertiti got ill and died, her body was [embalmed] quickly and taken to a secret location in a cave in the Desert.

Death of Akhenaten

I left a strong military presence in Thebes, and went back

to Amarna, to inform Akhenaten of the situation in Thebes. He left immediately for Thebes to see Nefertiti and calm the people, but his presence made things worse. People thought he was responsible for the gods' anger, many continued to die. He decided to go back to Amarna and wait there for this storm to pass, but he got ill too and died within a short time. He was embalmed quickly and taken to the secret location where Nefertiti was buried.

A Regency: Ay

I made offerings to Amun[76] and reopened the temple at Karnak. Returned to Amarna, and when the disease had disappeared, things slowly returned to normal. Ay[77] took care of the royal children, and I of the country. When it was safe, we abandoned Amarna and returned to Thebes after a few years, when harvest was good and granaries were full again. I asked- 'Why did you hack off images and cartouches of Akhenaten?' Horemheb replied:

'People were angry, we had to do something to calm them and the gods. By removing them, we felt we cleansed the Kingdom of their anger.

I was a loyal supporter, though I did not agree with some of his policies.

I was loyal, I served two Kings, I was loyal to them, I served them well.

I have spoken, I have spoken, I have spoken'.

156.A Beautiful City a Beautiful Man

'I saw a beautiful white city stretched out in the desert in the strong sunlight, against a deep blue sky, an aerial view: Amarna in all its glory. I also saw Akhenaten wearing his rounded crown[104], beautiful features, dark soft eyes like Tutankhamun's, athletic and perfectly formed[105]not deformed, perhaps in his late twenties, riding his chariot through the streets.' [24.9.16]

187.Palace Buildings

The Palace is a vast complex of mudbrick buildings opening on courtyards with pools and flowerbeds and trees to provide shade and coolness in the heat of the day.

There are the Princesses' quarters, the King's quarters, the Queen's quarters, all with their own large servant quarters; the courtiers' quarters with their own servant quarters, and so on. It is a vast complex of beautifully arranged buildings. In its heart lies the Temple where Akhenaten performs his rites to the Sun God. He alone can do this. He is the incarnation of the Sun God and therefore a God himself. By worshipping him, people worship the Sun God. [17.1.18]

Simmering Unrest

There is harmony in the Royal Court, although there are deep currents of opposition there and all over the country, where the Old Gods have been officially discarded and neglected.

208.Trying to connect

Last night I had the beginning of a panic attack which fortunately did not materialize. I will try to uncover what is causing it.

'Immediately, there is a soreness around the heart chakra. Akhenaten is slowly emerging from the mists of Time, tall, slender, wearing the Crown of Upper Egypt [?], and a knee-long tunic with short sleeves.'

Very slow-moving session, tried for nearly two hours, but could not access this Life. [4.7.21]

211.A Royal Father Always a Father

Yesterday, at about 7 pm, I felt the onset of a panic attack. This has never happened so early in the day, usually late at night, early morning. I will try to discover this Life which has been bothering me for months.

'I am a Pharaoh, wearing the rounded Crown, it is early morning. I am in Amarna. It is the start of a beautiful day. The sky is clear, the sun is rising, life is emerging from the sleep of night. Everything is peaceful, in the distance the sound of a wild dog barking.

This is a beautiful city, with a large central avenue, smaller streets radiating from this central artery. Neat, clean homes for its people. I am proud of this city I have created, of the large gardens, the pools of cooling waters, the palm trees, the plants, the flowers.

The Sun is rising high into the sky and I raise my arms to receive its blessings. Soon, I will perform the morning rites to the Sun God, the Aten, and then will ride my chariot through the city to bless its people.

We are a loving Family. We love Our Children. But life is hard, even for a Sun God. We lost a Daughter, and sorrow hit Us hard. The Palace became a place of Sorrow. I retired further into myself, in close communication with my Father, the Aten. I became more remote, cut-off from my people, let the Empire take care of itself. Horemheb was a trusted, very capable, Army Commander-in-Chief. I had Visions. I immersed myself into worshipping the Sun God.

Slowly, we recovered from Our Daughter's death, life returned to normal, but the pain of her loss remained deep into Our hearts. We greatly loved Our Children, Our little Sun Gods. I still feel that pain now, as I sit here and write this. The sight of that lifeless little Body was too much to bear for Us. Our grief was great.'

I feel this pain as it takes over my body and hits me hard, as I rock to and fro in my chair. It is overpowering, colossal, far reaching. It reminds me of another, all- pervading Sorrow at the early death of one of my two Sons Centuries later, in my life as a General in Rome, which I also still feel today.

'Darkness fell over Us and the Royal Children were devastated. They did not understand Death. I feel Pain in my heart, this great, great, Pain. One Misfortune followed another. Plague and Drought struck the Empire. Our Father, the Nile, was low, the fields were dry and bare, the granaries empty.

The Wind of Discontent blew over the Country. There is widespread unrest. I see crowds of starving people in the streets, menacing, forcing the Temples to open. We send some of Our foodstuff through the Empire, but it is not enough. People are dying. Children are dying, their thin bodies feed the hungry, mad, crowds.

I worship the Aten to rescue Us all. Nefertiti is dead. I am alone. I struggle to find meaning in my life, feel my God has abandoned me. I sit on my Throne staring vacantly in front of me, waiting for news. I am overwhelmed with Sorrow, cannot bear it.

Nefertiti's Body is brought back to Amarna. Oh, the Pain of Her death! Oh, the stillness of that Body, once so full of life! All is collapsing around me. I wait for developments. In this weakened state, I catch the plague and die. Death was quick, I did not linger. I feel my life was an unfinished business. I lost what I loved most.'

I feel the weight of this Pain, this Sorrow, heavy on my heart. I am tired. This Regression has lasted nearly two hours, I am exhausted. I want to close. Akhenaten is still here, though, does not want to go away. Have something to say?

'Nefertiti was the love of my life' he whispers. Great sadness over his face. 'I had other minor wives but although I loved them, they were nothing to me. She was the life of my life. I am glad I died shortly after Her. We were brought together to a secret location in the Desert, side by side, as we were in life.' I feel the intensity ofhis sorrow, but I close, too tired. '[15.11.21]

Chapter 5

Roman Egypt

2.Roman Invasion

'I SEE THE Valley of the Kings, a Roman General with a dark-red mantle, the sun is shining, he is holding the Pharaoh. In the background soldiers with banners and spears, an army marching. Awesome. I see them from below, as if I am under their feet, a Roman Army.

Scenes of Egyptian Life

I see the Nile at the back surrounded by palm trees. Quite a peaceful scene. The water is very clear and calm. There is a bend in the river, a quiet corner with some shadow provided by the trees, and some people sitting on the river banks. Lush vegetation. A lovely girl with brown eyes, her head covered by some cloth-she must be very young, a lovely little face, nice little teeth. Her mouth is open in a kind of smile. She is dressed all in white-she is all covered. Reeds are all around and the water is very calm and smooth, very peaceful.

I see the head of a Pharaoh in the background, the Valley of the Kings in the Desert, the Sphinx's beautiful face and eyes. Egyptian women dressed in white at the entrance of the Temple, the columns are white shining under the sun, pearly hair combed up in slightly Greek/Roman fashion'. [11.11.92]

5.Thebes: A Love Story

'There is a Temple carved in the rock with long steps going down. I am with a young pharaoh. He takes me by the hand and we go through a passage and we are outside in the Valley of the Kings. The sun is shining and the light is very powerful. He looks around and still holds me by the hand. We go down the steps into the Valley, walking on the hot sand. There is another man, a tall man, confronting us, wearing a small crown rounded at the edges[2], like a triangle, but not quite a triangle. My companion is clutching my hand very tight.

I do not know what is happening.

All three of us are quite young, late teens. There seems to be an argument between the two men and the one who was holding me so tight throws me into the arms of the other man who embraces me and kisses me on the face and the other one who was holding me before looks dejected and is walking away.

I do not know what is going on.

He is looking at me, he is much taller than me, he is looking down at me and holds me in his arms, he is lifting me in his arms and is carrying me. I put my arms around his neck and rest my head on his shoulder as he is carrying me in his arms to rest in the shadow of the Pyramid. I see the face of the Sphinx in the sunshine. He is gently putting me on the ground to rest and he is with me and taking care of me, he sits by me and I rest my head on his shoulder as I sit on his knees. He bends down to kiss me on the lips. There is great peace around us, a feeling of peace and eternity. He is staring into the sky and I am sitting on his knees looking at his face. He turns towards me again, bends over and kisses me again and we are lost in thoughts as we lie on the sand for a long time and fall asleep. At dusk, the golden light spreads all over the desert and the sky is all red and beautiful with all this beautiful light. We wake up and we get up and hand in hand we move away from the Pyramid. There is a camel waiting for us. He lifts me up on top of the camel and sits in front of me and I embrace him and we move away gently. The camel walks very gently, very softly, on the sand and all around us there is this glorious feeling of eternity, this beautiful sky, this feeling of immortality.

We are very happy together. I put my arms around him and

he is driving the camel, we approach the Palace and he stops the camel by the side of the Palace, gently takes me in his arms and places me down, he is very attentive.

He puts me on the steps on the side of the entrance and we walk into this Palace and some girls come and take me, but before leaving he comes close and bends over me and kisses me with a loving look in his eyes.

The servant girls take me away to change my dress and to refresh me and I am taken into a room made of marble with a pool in the middle, the pool is sunken into the floor, they undress me and I step into the water. It is a small pool. I feel quite safe and comfortable in the water. I am relaxing in the water and they bathe me and I look happy and relaxed and step out of the water. They dry me and put ointments on me and fresh beautiful light clothes, white veil on my hair. I have a very soft face, very white skin, very beautiful, soft, black eyes with a beautiful spiritual light in them. I am sitting on a stool in front of what looks like a dresser and I am lost in thoughts. Along come the girls and put a kind of dress with small wings on the shoulders going slightly up, and I feel now dressed with these clothes.

What is happening?

That Pharaoh has come back into my private apartment and has raised me in his arms, he is embracing me, seems very fond of me, seems unable to stay away from me, takes me close to his heart in a long embrace which gives me happiness and fills my heart with peace and serenity and he is resting his chin on my head as I rest my head against his chest. Another Pharaoh appears, he is older, perhaps in his middle thirties, not sure who he is, a serene look in his eyes, a good face, a bit long.

A Crisis

What is happening?

Someone is calling out of the room ‘Aretia’, ‘Aretia’, ‘Aretia’.

I do not know what is happening. There is heaviness in my heart. I do not know what is happening, there is confusion. I see this woman with this wig [do not know who she is], looks rather concerned, in front of me. Again, I hear a name, 'Aretia'.

I see a large room, two thrones in it, rather dark, very little light. I am sitting on the throne, but cannot see clearly. The room is huge, marble on the floor, lots of paintings on the walls, beautiful paintings. I see again the older Pharaoh, it feels as if there is some kind of crisis going on, not sure what that crisis is. I am sitting on a stool and look rather well… I stare in front of me, lost in thoughts. I see the face of a Pharaoh wearing a crown, there is some action just now, there is this feeling as if I am hanging on a thread waiting for something to happen and I do not know what it is that is going to happen, there does not seem to be any movement.

What is happening now?

A huge room again, with open windows and columns, a woman sitting, wearing a different crown. Again, I see the Temple with very tall columns into this huge square.

Roman Invasion and Surrender

What is happening?

I am not sure. There are Roman soldiers, someone assaulted, soldiers on steps, and suddenly on top of the stairs the tall Pharaoh and myself, he is holding me and embraces me, looking down on this Roman General coming up towards us. The General is talking to us inside the Temple, a very good-looking man, a very good face.

I do not know what is happening.

In the Temple, I am sitting on the throne, the Pharaoh is sitting in the other and we are listening to what the General has to say. Suddenly I see the three of us outside the Temple and in the square and this General is talking to the Priests and his hands are raised into the air. We are there all dressed in white. There are Roman soldiers coming into the square and filling the square up, in armours and shields, and then they go with the priests and it is quite striking the contrast between the white robes of the priests and the reddish colour of the soldiers' armours and banners. Not sure what is happening, there is interference from another time period. Yet I see the Pharaoh looking down on the people from the balcony of the Palace, do not know what is happening now. The square is empty and the people have gone.

Conclusion

I see a Pharaoh, now he holds in his arms the lifeless body of his wife Aretia. I have a feeling that she killed herself. He is holding her, desperately looking at her face, she has gone and she is lifeless in his arms and he is putting her gently on the bed. Do not know what is happening now, he is desperate, I think he is going to kill himself…Some noise coming from a room and he is lying down on the bed close to her, side by side, embracing her body and suddenly he is gone [poison?]' [21.2.93]

21.Roman General-A Foreign Land

'I saw a Roman General-a tall, good-looking, athletic man in his 40s–wearing a crown of laurels, a dark-brown breastplate armour on a short white tunic, a red mantle fastened on his right shoulder, and knee-high sandals. I was a successful governor of a foreign land and helped the local people by kindness to understand the new things which Rome brought with its conquests. I rejoice in this Roman life. I was happy and spread kindness.' [8.6.98]

72.Visions of Egypt

'At the start of a long regression Sekhmet[46] appeared and remained with me for a long time, and then the effigy of an Egyptian woman [on a coffin?] I saw a young Egyptian man, possibly about 30 years old, with long, dark-brown wavy hair and moustache, very good-looking, like actor Omar Sharif when he was young, wearing a long white tunic with long sleeves and sandals, walking on the golden-yellow sand in the desert. I saw him from above, looking down on him. Do not know who he is.

Marc Anthony

Then a Roman General with a thick short black beard and moustache, in full armour and helmet, on a horse, and another Roman General, again in armour and helmet and I felt I was that

General, sitting in my chair with the full weight of his armour on my body. I saw Roman houses from above, with red-tiled roofs, a building with columns, the Senate, a Senator, Julius Caesar, wearing a white toga.

Octavian-Cleopatra

I saw a statue of the Emperor Octavian[47] and the Roman General again. I caught a glimpse of a woman with a Ptolemaic nose and light-coloured curly hair, Cleopatra.

Marc Anthony's Death-30 BC

The Roman General was Marc Anthony[48]. I slowly went into his pain, with difficulty at first, as if there was no pain, or little of it, but I persisted and felt a terrible pain, very deeply seated, hitting my solar plexus.

'I suddenly felt the full impact of a thrust into my stomach, so strong that I bent down as the sword entered the stomach and the tip came out on the back, so strong was the thrust. Marc Anthony was not ready to go when he killed himself, still in the prime of life, full of ambition.' The memory of that Life still haunts me today. 'I also saw a young Roman man perhaps 20 years old, with a golden ring across his head, wearing a short red-brick tunic and gold sandals - Octavian.' [1.8.13]

Chapter 6

Imperial Rome

42.Claudius[18][AD 41-54]

'I REGRESSED TO a Roman Life. I was wearing sandals, a tunic, a gold crown, and there were buildings and pillars around me, Rome. I went to the Senate and sat on a throne there was a Roman General next to me, wearing helmet, armour, a mantle, and he was looking/speaking to me. I moved forward in time. I was wearing armour. I was 35 years old, tall, slender, good- looking, manly. I saw a beautiful Mediterranean coast, sea merging with the sky, as if seen from above. I had a family, a wife, whom I saw, children. The lesson I learnt in that Life was Commitment: to loved ones, to work, to responsibilities, to my goals. My name was Claudius. I was a Roman Emperor.' [24.5.2009]

43.An Important Roman Life [5thCentury BC]

'I was Flavia, wife of a Roman Consul, 5th Century BC, good-looking, in armour, a man of importance.'

78.Octavian [63 BC-August 14 AD]

'I saw a young man in his early 30s, good-looking, with short, wavy, blond hair and a laurel crown on his head, sitting, wearing a long white tunic and a long mantle. I felt I was him, Octavian. On his left side, there was a white building with columns, like a Greek temple, on top of white steps [the Senate?]

and white Roman houses. I also saw a young Octavian in a knee-long, sleeveless, dark red-rust tunic and an older one in armour.

Roman General

44.The Desert

Before I started this regression, I felt very sad and did not know why. 'I saw a Roman General standing by a tall and narrow, arch between two columns. He looked in the distance, lost in his thoughts and was alone.' I felt great sadness and intense pain.

'I then saw him riding a horse, a silhouette against the yellow sky, very sunny and hot, the desert. Isaw him again, perhaps in his late 40s. He had a long, dry, manly face and short, blond, hair. He was wearing a white tunic and toga[19] and a crown of laurels on his head. He was sitting on a throne, lost in his thoughts, deep dark eyes.'

Rome: Civil War [31 BC]

I felt his great pain, his sadness and his sorrow weighing heavily on his heart. I was him. I got a faint 'Year 31 BC'[20] but nothing else. The pain was still there and would not go away. 'I saw him as a young man in Rome. He had beautiful, short, curly, black hair. He was wearing armour and sandals, no helmet. Streets crowded with people, buildings like temples with many columns. I saw the Roman Army marching. AWSOME.' [24.2.13]

52.Julius Caesar [July 100-March 44 BC]

There is always a restless feeling of unfulfillment, of sadness and sorrow which I cannot explain and cannot get rid of. A short meditation brought me back to Roman times. 'I saw a Roman General[29] with plumed helmet, armour and cloak. I saw the Senate, senators, Julius Caesar[29]-he was exactly like his statues, he had a most remarkable face and pale-blue eyes. Saw the interior of a Roman patrician house–a woman[wife?] and daughter [or young boy?]. I was that Roman General. He was very athletic and attractive. I was wearing his clothes and sandals, but did not discover how he died, or 'who' he was, although I felt I was also dressed in a white tunic and had a crown of laurels on my head. I was very sick as I approached the end of that Life, but could not get to the death scene.' [24.6.13]

58.Two Sons Two Lives

This Life regularly comes up, there is a deeply buried sorrow and trauma which refuses to reveal itself and is another source of disquiet and restlessness. 'A Roman General appeared in all his glory: plumed helmet, red cloak, beautiful armour, long leather sandals, sword. Saw a teenage boy with short, curly, brown hair, wearing a short white tunic. Saw him later in his life when he was 19 and in his early 20s. Beautiful young man. I then saw another young man, black hair, slightly aquiline nose, beautiful black eyes, looking at me, wearing a white tunic. Very attractive. I saw him in his 20s wearing armour and the Roman General again, the black-haired youth as an old man, lying on his back, dead, wearing a white tunic'. I felt a very deep pain in the solar plexus, covering the chest and throat. These people were all of very high standing, though I do not know who they are. I could not get the last thought and feeling before death. [11.7.13]

60.A Proud Father

A very upsetting, two-hour long regression.

'I was a Roman General in full armour, a very good looking and tall man in his early 30s. I saw a beautiful young man, perhaps 20/22-years old, with short, black, curly hair and large black eyes, tall and well built, in a short white tunic; the Roman General on a horse leading his legions; and an old Senator sitting in the Senate. Saw a very beautiful young man who looked like my teenage friend, with blond, wavy short hair; tall, athletic, wearing a short white tunic, like the Greek God Apollo, his face close to mine, probably 22 years old; a white building with columns on top of a long flight of steps.

Death of a Much-Loved Son

I saw the Roman General in his 40s, myself, deep lines on his face, looking worried, kneeling over the dead body of the young blond-haired man. I felt the impact of this man's sorrow first in my solar plexus, but it was so overpowering that it reached the heart and the crown chakras. How did he die?

I saw an extremely beautiful young woman, about 30 years old or slightly over, with masses of dark, chocolate- brown hair with shades of red, combed back up Roman style; oval face, white skin, large chocolate-brown eyes, wearing a long, white tunic.'

I picked up tremendous sadness, very, very deep, vast like an ocean, so total and vast that it had no boundaries, it was all pervasive, it stretched over the sky and beyond. It was so strong I thought it would break me apart. I thought of the Roman family, of the brothers Gracchi[39], but I do not think it was them I saw. I did not get any details of their situation, only the terrible sorrow and sadness of his death. During the regression, I felt a strong pain in the sole of my left foot and the palm of my left hand, the whole left side of my body was badly affected. I was upset for weeks. [20.7.13]

66.A Vestal

'Suddenly, out of nowhere, this very beautiful young woman with a very Byzantine face came to me, with rich hazelnut hair, oval face and very good figure, wearing a sleeveless dress, pleated, with high-chest belt. I thought she was a Vestal of the Temple of Vesta in Rome.'[41]

Roman Emperor and General

'From higher up, looking down, I saw a white Roman city, very beautiful in the sunshine, with white marble tops, and a Roman

General in glorious armour, very athletic and very good looking.

I also caught a glimpse of a Roman Emperor in armour, sitting, and a building with columns on his left side, wearing a crown of laurels and felt I was that Emperor and that General.

Jesus Christ [d AD 30-33]

Then, suddenly, Jesus Christ appeared to me wearing white tunic and mantle, his head covered with white cotton cloth, but with a crown of thorns underneath. He had a black, short beard and moustache. Then I saw Jesus as he appears in Catholic tradition, blond-red hair and white tunic, a red heart surrounded by a halo of Light.

I saw the Roman General again and felt very strong, overpowering, pain in my solar plexus. I was not told the nature of this ancient trauma, but it was overpowering. I had a feeling that the Roman General helped Jesus carry the Cross, later, when He was crucified'.

Although the Roman General was in Palestine and in his 30s at that time, when Jesus appears in Past Lives it can also mean that something terrible is going to happen to someone and that they too, like Christ, will undergo their Calvary and carry their own Cross on their shoulders: the weight of their deep traumas and sorrows. In this case, the death of a much-loved son, the effects of which I still feel to this day. [24.7.13]

75.A Roman Family

'Again, I saw a Roman General in a very beautiful armour and helmet, very shiny, like silver, with a long, thick, sumptuous mantle. I saw an old Senator [perhaps 60 years old] with a long white toga and the Senate behind him, a building with columns, like a temple. Then a beautiful Roman lady appeared with thick, dark-brown hair; and a girl or a boy. I saw the Roman General again, without helmet, a beautiful head of thick, short wavy hair, rich dark-brown, good looking and athletic'. I suddenly felt a deep-rooted pain in the solar plexus twisting my stomach and felt sick.

97.Roman General And I

'I was a Roman General, wearing helmet, armour, cloak, sandals, sword. We were facing one another and I offered him my hand.' I felt the impact of his trauma and immense sorrow but could not release them. [1.4.15]

143.An Unexpected Revelation

Early this morning while still in bed, I had a tremendous insight. All week I felt a great sadness, pain and sorrow, which made me ill. I realized that my teenage friend who died tragically when he was about 22 years old was one of the Roman General's boys in a Past Life which kept coming up, and I was that Roman General, his father, and my sorrow at his early death is the Roman General's sorrow stretching out into modern times, still unresolved.

A Teenage Friend

59.Brief Encounters - A Very Special Soul

'I saw a long-lost teenage friend, a very beautiful boy who looked like the Greek God Apollo.[37] He died in his very early twenties in tragic circumstances. His memory and sorrow at his early death have never left me. Then, Nefertiti[38] emerged from the mists of Time.' [16.7.13]

69.A Pain That Never Goes Away - A Flashback

'My teenager Friend appeared, tall, blond, short curly hair. Manly features, smiling.'

The memory of his death brought back immense sadness and sorrow. My Grandfather was with me all the time, to support me in my grief. [29.7.13]

Roman Battles

75.A Battle - The Aftermath

'Saw him on a horse, in battle, bodies scattered all over the battlefield surrounded by trees, on top of each other. I was hit in the stomach by a long spear [like those of the Greek Hoplites].' However, I am not sure that that is how I died and I could not get the last thought.' [9.8.13]

98.Memories - A Roman Home-A Battle

'I became a beautiful young Roman man [perhaps 22 years old] with short wavy blond hair, looking like the actor Keith Ledger, wearing armour. I saw a building like the Senate; then his home, a patrician building with large atrium [courtyard] servants going to and fro. Saw him at the head of the Roman Army leading his legions through a large passage through trees [forest], then a battle in a field. Next, he was sitting on a throne [?] wearing a crown of laurels and a white tunic.' Could not discover who he was and could not go to the death scene. I felt something stir in my stomach which shrank forcefully as it shot up to my throat chakra, but did not exit. However, the heaviness and the pain in the heart area disappeared and I felt much lighter and breathed better. [18.5.15]

106.Battle of Teutoburg Forest [AD 9[78]]

'Saw the Roman Senate and the statue of a general, an emperor [?], white marble, myself as a Roman General, helmet, armour, sandals, mantle, sitting in my chair as I write this.

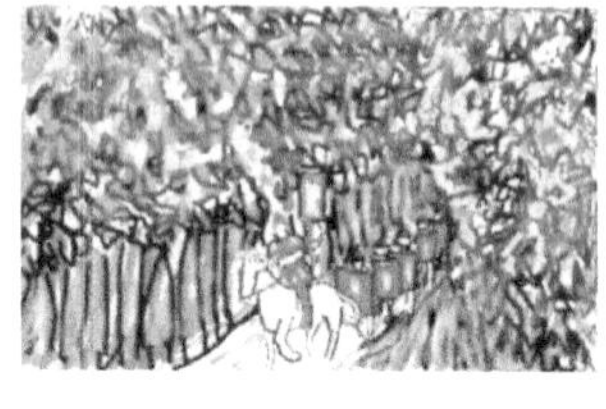

There is a wood, a forest, with a narrow passage surrounded by trees, soldiers marching not in their usual formations but broken up in twos or threes, the path being too narrow for more men. It is a trap.

As they walk forward, bands of tribesmen drop on them, they fight back, but many are killed. Manymanage to get through to an open field where they are confronted by more enemies. A blond-haired man with moustache and short beard stands out, a 'Barbarian' [Arminius], 'Germania' comes to mind. The Romans fight them back, but many more are killed. It is a tragedy, a carnage. They manage to bury most of the Fallen in the field, but those killed in the wood remain unburied, they are too many and cannot be transported in the field, nor buried in the wood.

The General is overcome with emotion and cries out aloud, lamenting the death of his legions. How many? I ask. 'Too many, fifteen/twenty thousand men? A massacre'. I cry a lot, I feel the General's sorrow, very, very deep. 'Germania' echoes through.

'Back in Rome the General is an old man. I see him dead, but cannot get his last thought, nor whether his Soul went into the Light. I think he died naturally, but with a heavy heart. He felt responsible for his men, their Souls still probably in the wood, only some of them going towards the Light. I saw a white shape going up towards the Light, the Roman General?' [28.5.15]

Chapter 7

Palestine

170.Roman General - A Timeless Land

'I FOUND IT difficult to connect, but I am sinking down, deep, deep down. I have arrived. I am a man about 30 years old, shoulder length black hair, short beard and moustache, good-looking. I am wearing a white tunic and sandals, I am tall. There is sand around me: where am I?

I see a Roman General on a horse, it is very hot, very sunny. Where am I? Palestine comes through. I see small houses scattered here and there in the desert, the distant outline of the sea. The sky is very blue in the midday sun. I see small oases, camels, caravans crossing the desert. I stare intensely at some point in the distance, and so is the Roman General. I see ancient villages where Life runs slow, palm trees.

175.A Building Made of Light

'I find myself walking down a long corridor, softly lit, with many doors. I open one and a wave of soft light envelops me. It is all foggy, like being in a cloud, dense cloud, white cloud.

I walk softly forward, though I do not know in which direction. I am wearing a long, white tunic made of air, my hair is long. I realise I am in Spirit, dead. I must be, to be here. The clouds are very light grey and they move softly as I walk through them. I wonder where I am going. My Third Eye pierces the thickness of the mist, like a search light. I feel the light pressure of hands on my shoulders, someone is behind me. There is a

Presence. I feel dizzy as I stand on these clouds.

In the distance, there is a Building made of Light, like a castle with turrets. I am there in a large Hall. It has no substance. I go through its walls. I wonder what it is all about. I stand there, not knowing what to do. Suddenly, a flash of Light opens up a passage and I walk through it. Someone is right behind me, hands on my shoulders. I feel pressure on my chest, something struggling to come up, to be released. I do not see anything at all now. A soft Darkness surrounds me, but the Presence is with me. I am not afraid. Something pushes up from deep inside.

Horatio Carnelli

I see the face of a man, possibly around 40, long curly black hair, with a round, chubby face, large black eyes, thick eyebrows and lips, smallish round nose, not attractive, but pleasant. Who is he?

Like me, he wears a tunic made of cloud. Again, there is a strong, upward push from the solar plexus. This man is here with me, very close, on my right-hand side, his face nearly touching mine. I tell him I want to stop soon. The other Presence is still behind me so there are two of them. He has a chubby face, but slim of body.

Are you Horatio Carnelli, a doctor who lived at the time of Christ? I ask. This memory suddenly came to me. Why are you here? I am puzzled. Again, there is an upward movement inside me. I want to close and tell him to hurry up. Weird. There is an Outline of a Body of Light stretched out on what looks like a narrow table with something like a thin mattress on it. Who is that? I ask.

This man is right in front of me.

There is a strong White Light all around. I am covered with White Light, like standing under a shower of White Light. This man is now younger and rather fat.

A Village in Palestine

I see a village in Palestine, time of Christ. Palm trees, very strong light, but there is a cooling shadow under a porch in one house. It is all very peaceful. Some children play in a corner, a couple of donkeys in another, women making bread. The Desert under the scorching sun. It is beautiful. All is as it should be. Or is it?' I feel agitated and close the session.

Central America [1200 BC]

37.Two Lives

A long regression took me back to Central America a long time ago [1200 BC]. 'From the mists of Time emerged a face, then a head, then the whole figure of a man with very good, delicate features, an Indio, slim, tall, naked to the waist. He was wearing some white pants and a short band-like headdress, keeping his hair back, with very short plumage around it.

A Tribal Leader

I was that man. I was a tribal leader, a warrior, and a strong man. I was involved with the Olmec tribes[113]. I faced a terrible threat from another tribe, the betrayal of one close family relative who wanted to take control of the group, and the hardest choice to make: what punishment to give him. I meditated to the great Sun God for many hours and eventually I made my decision.

It was my brother who had betrayed me. My advisors and priests wanted him to be killed as a traitor. Fortunately, they did not ask for him as sacrifice to the Gods, for one chosen for this purpose was sacred and I could not have fought it. His betrayal was cruel, but for my mother and so I sent them both and his family [but for his family I gave them choice to go or stay as they were not involved] into exile. As it happened, they all went, but one daughter who loved me as a father stayed and became part of my family. With this decision, I rested easy for it was a great crime to cause the death of a close family member in this time and I had been placed in a near impossible position. I made the right choice of how to deal with people who were a danger to me, who used my trust and sense of honour to manipulate me, but as a family I had to work out a solution without killing or sacrifice. I was revered and honoured.'

An Artist and a Shaman

'In the Life immediately after, I was a designer of complex pictures used in the art of my people-face and body painting in Neolithic times. These marks stated my family and my work as a Shamanic dream-caller. They were all marks of power and more were added as I attained more knowledge. They were seen as beautiful and enhanced me in the eyes of my people. I wove the mysteries and spiritual beliefs in subtle and symbolic form into all my work. I had a long and dedicated Life and was greatly respected by my family and fellow artists.'

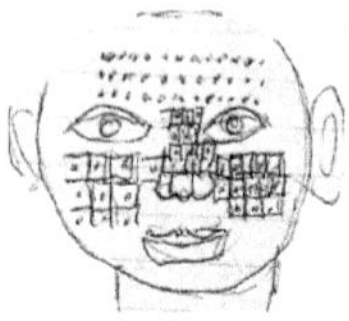

Persia [Ancient Iran]

10.Fear of Enclosed Spaces

'A Life from Susa.[6]' I did not get details from that Life, but only experienced an overwhelming fear of suffocation and panic connected with small spaces, perhaps imprisoned in a small cell for life. Horrible feeling.

Anatolia [Southern Turkey]

10.Life in the Taurus Mountains[5]

'I was writing words as someone dictated them–cuneiform writing. They do not feel true. I question the meaning of the words and I am flung from a high tower for daring to question them.' As a result, I have suffered all my life from a crippling fear of heights, fear of falling. [21.11.96]

Ancient Greece

17.A Burial A Long Time Ago

'There is a burial, 3000 years ago–Greece? Turkey? I am weeping by the memorial, my husband was a fine man, and I am afraid of the future.' [20.5.97]

92.A Very Beautiful Land

I did two and a half hour's regression which only partly succeeded. 'There was a beautiful land by the sea-Greece in ancient times, a mountain sloping down to the sea, an intensely azure sky. I was struck by the beauty of the colour of the sea, so vivid, and the paler colour of the sky, as if in a light mist. The sea was on the left side of the scene, and to the right, in the sparsely green covered mountain, an amphitheatre with very white columns which stood out against the overwhelmingly azure of the landscape.

I saw a young man, perhaps 30 years old, tall, attractive, with short, curly, dark-blond hair with shades of gold, moustache and short beard, very Greek features, wearing a white tunic. I was this man and felt an overwhelming sadness and pain weighting heavily on my chest. I wondered what could have happened to him in such fantastic surroundings, what could possibly have gone wrong? Towards the end of the session, suddenly the Patriarch[61] came to me, dressed in black, black hat, black hair, moustache and beard, and also a young man in his mid-30s, can see him very well, but do not knowwhy he came to me'. He is still here as I write this. [16.7.14]

Africa And India

10.Fears in The Blood

A long Regression brought up different Lives and Time periods and the fears associated with them.

Fear of Big Animals

I always wondered why I cannot go to the zoo, because of my uncontrollable terror of big animals [elephants, lions, rhinos] until 'I had a glimpse of two Past Lives, one in Africa and one in India. I was mauled by lions.' [4.6.96]

Chapter 8

Middle Ages

25.A Miner [600 years ago] A Happy Outcome

'I WAS WORKING in a mine. Light-coloured dust drifting, setting on my hair and clothes. I wonder what I am doing here. I have suddenly woken up and come to myself and realized I have left my home and family far away. I want to visit my parents again. I make the decision to travel to see them–good fortune awaits me when I arrive there. This was 600 years ago.' [11.7.98]

31.Burnt Alive: A Nasty Memory

'I saw myself on a fire pyre still alive. This Life was a few centuries ago. I refused to give myself to a powerful man, because I loved another and he did not wish me to be with anyone but him. He told lies about me and incited others against me until one day a mob seized me and put me on the pyre. It was unfair and unjustified. It was in Italy, borders area. The man who caused my death went on to take more community control, but those he worked with saw how he manipulated events and people, and he began to be distrusted. My lover was distraught. He left and walked around for seven years scraping a living and then joined a monastery and gained comfort from walking in the garden and seeing the seasons change around him.

The man who caused my death ignored his actions for many years. He married and had four children. People gradually started to fear him and he became a more powerful landowner.

He was not punished for his crime, there was no evidence against him and he was not blamed. I was the one he blamed for many things. Karma does not always happen immediately. He carried on as he was. That personality type would not have been able to learn this lesson. He realized when it was too late to even admit he was at fault-this was partly his punishment which, at the time, was not great. He was an evil man and his punishment was greater later. No-one liked him. He was greedy and rapacious. He did not find love in marriage, if anything, he became more power-crazed and self- obsessed. In that Life, he could ignore his own actions, but in the Life after he remembered and all he could see was the pyre and feel love and guilt. He became a religious man and punished himself again and again, never forgiving himself. He lived through this for seven years of silence and total suffering.' This, however, was of little comfort to me and did not diminish the feeling of extreme anger which got hold of me for several days. [26.5.99]

71.Erasmus Da Rotterdam [1466-1536]

'I saw a 16th century man, Erasmus da Rotterdam[42], in priestly clothes and hat similar to those worn by Thomas Cranmer,[43] Archbishop of Canterbury in the 1530s. He looked like the young Erasmus, but had a slightly shorter, slightly aquiline nose, or so I thought, a very square face, particularly the jaw; very hollow cheeks, dark piercing eyes.

103.Richard the Lionheart [157-1199]

Did one-and-a-half-hour regression, a bit chaotic.

'I saw a tall man, with reddish-blond hair, short, thick beard, thick moustache and eyebrows, strong face, in his early 30s, with a small round crown. He was wearing a long-tunic-like robe with ermine on his shoulders. At first, I did not know who he was. I thought he was a Russian Tsar. I then saw a lion and thought 'Richard the Lionheart[72]' I saw him for some time, but could not go any further.

154.An Avalanche-An Untimely Death

Feelings of fear and suffocation preceded this regression.

'The avalanche is overtaking me as I am running on a mountain or hill side, just outside a city in a North Mediterranean country-Italy or Greece. I am pinned down by stones. I am hopeless and unable to move. Breathing is difficult. There is enormous pressure on the lungs, making it harder and harder to breathe. I am struggling to escape, but my strength is not enough. I stay alive through the night and can just see the sky and the moon pass overhead. I fear dying at night, it reminds me of a dream I had as a child and believe that my soul will be hurt by creatures of the night. I manage to survive till morning when the sun comes into the sky and I see the sunrise colours. I slip into death, but feeling safe and protected by the daylight.

I am a young girl, only in my teenage years and quite beautiful too. It seems so sad. I think of all the things I will not be able to do before I die.' A strong feeling this happened in the Middle Ages. [4.4.16]

Chapter 9

In The Monastery

8.Many Lives Many Roles

'A LIFE WHEN I died for my faith. My refusal to look at the new brought me death.' 'Life as a nun in the convent. I developed the Stigmata for a few weeks. I was amazed at the holes in my hands and the gushing blood which vanished into air as it fell, while instantly reappearing.' 'A Life as an actor–man in drag-female role in Ancient Greece.' 'A Roman Life, very early in Palestine, as a questioning, demanding wife - husband felt frustrated because he could not answer or do what I wanted.' 'Another Life, late in European History, as a demanding child always wanting more, never satisfied with toys that were given.' 'Also, saw a man in drag–contemporary.' [28.3.96]

9.Lives as a Nun-11th-13th century Italy

'I saw three Popes and myself as a nun. In that Life, I modelled myself on a teacher who taught control over the body. I learnt to see the body as the servant of the Spirit and did not appreciate it for the experiences it could bring to me. Pope Urban was my teacher. We were distant relations–I was younger than he and a cousin. He chose the convent for me and put me there. He realized I was not happy but did not advise me to leave. He sought my forgiveness and understanding that my actions in that Life caused me frustration. I was so young and so cruel to myself, because I forced myself to stay in a situation which gave me no joy or happiness. I believed it was all for the greater good and that it was wrong to be happy. This is how I justified that Life to myself. I also had links with the other two Popes: Innocent III[3] and Boniface VIII[4] They still influence me today. They were all rigid authoritarians, disciplinarians. In those times, I also lived as a nun, one as the years turned to 1200, the other as the years turned to 1300 AD.' [11.4.96]

11.Jerome-A Difficult Legacy

'I was called Jerome and I was a priest learning and working with healing animals. I felt their suffering at the cruelty people inflicted on them and internalized it. It became part of myself.' And it still is so today.

14.Many Lives as a Nun Not All Happy

'Images of Lives in religious orders. Again, how difficult it is for me. I am young, I want to dance, but I cannot, because of my vocation. Feelings of frustration and lack of achievement in life.' [5.2.97]

18.More Lives as a Nun

'A Life of Silence and Privation.
I loved intensely, but believed my feelings were sinful.
Had I but known he loved me too!' [25.6.97]

27.Catholic Church Inquisition[116][15th Century]

'I saw myself as a nun visiting people in prison, in very basic conditions. I talk to them and comfort them. They feel much better and I am able to get through to most of them, although with some it takes quite a while. One day I know one of the prisoners, he was a priest from a nearby community. I talk to him and he explains how he has been persecuted for some of his learning and knowledge. He asks me to get a message through to another priest whom he fears will be next-that he must destroy some of his books, papers. I say I will try to help, but am troubled by the responsibility and do not know what to do. This leaves me in a state of mental turmoil, agitation and total fear. This Life was in the 15th century.' [14.12.98]

35.A Short Life

'I was a nun, living in a monastery and fell from a high wall and broke a rib. I still carry the scar of that accident. I caught a fever and death was marked by interludes of great pain - the body tortured and strained into wrong position. I was 32 years old. I was doing much good in the local community-caring for people and their animals, whom so often they left to suffer. By my words and actions, I was making people aware of treating their animals with respect.' [9.3.2000]

140.A Modern-Day Nun

Before I regressed, a modern-day Nun in short white dress came to me. A rather long face, in her early 50s. Do not know who she is-still here as I write. She is in front of Westminster Cathedral.

153.Life as a Nun with a twist in Spain

Before I started this regression, I felt extremely irritable and angry for no apparent reason. It all became clear as I unravelled this Past Life as a nun. 'In that Life, my family put me in a convent. They did not approve of the man I had fallen in love with. With my lover, I ran away, we tried to marry but the priest told my parents, because they said they would give a reward and he did not marry us. When my parents arrived, my lover was arrested and they were arguing with me. I always thought he would come and rescue me from the convent, but he did not. I did not know that my parents had him banished from the country to prevent this happening-they never told me. All they told me was that he had found someone else and had never really cared for me. I felt betrayed and hurt and embittered throughout this life and I grew old before I should have through sadness and self-neglect. My lover tried to reach me, but failed many times, my parents sent false messages to him also saying I did not wish to see him and eventually he believed them and travelled around the world as a sailor on a trading vessel [he did not marry]. My parents did not wish me to marry him because he was beneath me in social status, he was not a good match for me, although I loved him, they doubted him. He was much poorer than me and my family, my parents were not bad people, they wanted me to make a good marriage and be well looked after, they were aristocracy and related to the royal family. This was in Spain.

I did not stay in the convent all my life, but left after some years and whilst in the convent I became old and embittered. When I left, I involved myself in good works with the needy and ill. My life after the convent was good. I lived briefly with my parents, but then moved out to a country house. I did marry eventually, but after my parents died and left me as a wealthy lady. I was their only child. I married a much younger man, very handsome and gallant, not rich, but he swept me off my feet and made me very happy in my last few years. My two lovers were both good, kind, sincere men and loved me dearly.

I was 47 when I married the younger man, he was 31. He loved me and made me happy because he wanted to be with me-money was not his motivation. I was beautiful still and did look younger than my years'. [3.4.16]

Chapter 10

13th Century China

148.The Great Wall of China

'I AM AN old Chinese man. I have a long, thin, white moustache falling down the sides of my mouth, and a thin, long beard. I am wearing a round, pointed, cap and long silk tunic with long sleeves. I am very old. I have high cheekbones and hollow cheeks.

The Mongols Are Coming

I see the Long Wall[103] sneaking through the mountains, misty skies, pale-blue with feather-light clouds; towers, warriors on the alert, many more are joining them from other fortresses, fever pitch preparations.

The Mongols are coming fast on their horses, like flies, we stand ready, our archers drawing their arrows. The sun is high in the sky, their vast numbers fill the valleys below like ants, moving fast. We wait for them, we are ready. We stand firm, we have no fear.

I am a much younger man now, in my forties. I wear an armour dotted with gold and I stand on the ramparts looking down at the enemy. My will is invincible: they will notpass. I survey their positions: they are approaching the Wall with their long ladders, their arrows thick like a swarm of locusts covering the sky. We allow their fury to explode, then, as they climb up the Wall, we rain stones and arrows on them, but some make it to the top and ferocious hand-to-hand combat ensues. They fall, their bodies blocking the walkway. We throw them over the Wall causing others to fall off their ladders and onto the ground with them. I pursue the enemy on horseback along the length of the Northern Wall. I am possessed of great strength and superhuman power: they will not pass. Our land is ours. My sword swings to the left and to the right, felling people like trees, mutilated bodies, severed heads and limbs litter the walkway, turning the bricks red. I feel this power. I descend like a fury on the enemy, my warriors fight with renewed strength. I am Supreme Commander and Supreme Ruler. I am a Warrior-they will not pass.

Hundreds of Mongols have reached the top, the fight is intense, brutal, to the death. For a moment, they overwhelm us, but reinforcements have come and turn our fortunes around. In the valleys, at the foot of the Wall, the enemy is fast retreating, they will return at night to collect their dead or leave them there for the birds of prey and other wild animals. I am an old man now, a long and thin white moustache falling down the side of my mouth, long white beard. The borders are secure, we had no further attacks, but the enemy is within though temporarily tamed.' I feel pain deep into my stomach. [19.1.16]

149.In the Thick of Battle

'I see an army, a cavalry. Men in armours with raised shoulders, like small wings, small round hats with a spear in the middle, long, thin moustaches falling on the sides of their mouths, thin pointed beards [Mongols?] their long spears drawn. Awesome.

I see a young warrior, possibly late 20s, early 30s in full armour, hair taken up in the middle of his head, attractive. I see a vast expanse of flat lands, no trees, very flat [Mongolia?] Very distant hills mark the line between the earth and the sky.

I am a man in my 40s, good features, thin moustache, short beard along the jaw line. I wear a small round hat, I am richly dressed with a large, dark-red flowing robe on my tunic. I sit in my palace next to a large window overlooking a large rectangular garden surrounded by low buildings, lost in my thoughts. Some attendants sit on my sides, a step lower.

I see a battle, fast riding horsemen, their long spears drawn, clashing violently with other horsemen. Many are transfixed and fall to the ground and are trampled over. Others are badly wounded and covered in blood, but still fight. It is carnage. Dead horses lie on their backs, their legs up in the air, trampled over by other horses. It is total chaos. The noise is deafening, the clash of the weapons, the screams, the blowing of horns. I feel tension in my stomach. I feel sick. My throat is thick and dry. I feel sick as the tension mounts. It is all or nothing.

I wear a beautiful, distinctive, armour, but no helmet, my hair is tied up in a loop on top of my head, I am attractive, in my late 30s, early 40s, thin moustache and short beard along my jaw line. I stand out from the mix of warriors. My stomach churns. I feel sick. I am in the thick of the battle, swinging to the left and to the right with my sword, felling people like trees. I feel sick. My solar plexus is tight, my mouth dry. The battle has been going on for hours. We trample over dead horses and bodies are scattered everywhere, the overwhelming stench of blood and death. I feel sick.' [20.1.16]

150.On the Attack-A Snapshot

'The scene of a battle in a large flat area. Mongols on horses, their long spears drawn, fast advancing, small round pointed hats with fur rim, pulled down to their eyes. My stomach is very tight.' [25.1.16]

152.Chinese-Japanese Women

'I am Chinese, a beautiful young woman wearing a sort of 'spiky' golden headdress, white make-up and red lipstick, a long, heavy-silk tunic with 'winged' shoulders, trousers, black shoes. I see the same woman in another life, but Japanese, richly dressed with a dark blue-black kimono with golden silhouettes of flowers, beautiful hair, wearing very white socks on golden sandals. Another woman has a strange hairstyle, hair done up in a flat, rectangular shape in the middle of the head, combed from back to front, dressed in heavy clothes and heavy mantle. Men wearing flat rectangular caps in the middle of their heads, also from back to front, pushed forward with bands on the side of their faces joining under their chins.' [14.2.16]

Chapter 11

Ancient Japan

41.Life at The Top Ripe with Sorrow

'I SAW A beautiful young woman wearing a beautiful, rich, kimono and then a young man, his hair tied up into an oval [like an egg] over his head and a fringe. He too was very richly dressed and I looked into his eyes and felt very hot. I was that man. I looked down to my feet and was wearing gold slippers on very white socks. I moved forward in time and saw another man, in his 30s, very beautifully and very richly dressed, with a loose coat over a tunic made of heavy silk of dark red and other colours with the same style of hair, tied up in the middle of his head into an oval shape. On top of the head there was something like a small round hat held by black ribbons on the sides of his face, joining under his chin. I think he was an emperor, and he was the young man I saw earlier and he was me. I went backward and forward a few years. I saw a child. I felt great oppression in the throat and heart chakras[129], perhaps his parents were murdered, I do not know, I could not see much.' [22.3.2009]

45.Samurai-A Pointless War

In this regression, three different men, from three different time periods, rushed towards me, all wanting to be first, an amazing experience.

'The Samurai[21] was serving a warlord whose relations were trying to steal his lands and possessions. There was a pointless land war. Pointless, because when the lord died, he had no children. His enemy and nephew whom he had been fighting took the land anyway. The Samurai gave all for his lord and died in a great battle for a cause which was forgotten and left no impact behind it. Before this, the Samurai had served his lord's father well, but when the father died, the reckless son initiated the war of no return. He sent the Samurai and others to their deaths.

He was in his prime, a man of 37 years.

He learned endurance and perseverance, but it was an unfulfilled and unsatisfactory Life'. [9.5.13]

86.First Samurai-A Life of Self Denial

A very long regression which brought up two Lives. 'His name was Tachaka. He was born to be a Samurai.[56]

I saw him on a horse leading a very long column of foot soldiers with an impenetrable look on his face, wearing a round metal hat with large rim, slowly proceeding over very narrow pathways around mountains.

Tachaka was a very complex man. Although good at this work -he learned a violent unloving, spiritual path of self-sufficiency - he often had a longing for a gentler and more creative life, but he persevered and followed the will of his lord. His parents loved him and knew he had other skills and loves, so they just encouraged him to take joy in these and to have these interests as hobbies.

Tachaka also learned to put his personal will aside and be of service to those the ancestors had placed above him. A great sense of hierarchy and spiritual obedience, strength of will and determination came from this time- some of these things are still present today in this Life.'

I asked why he did not change his profession and follow his dreams.

'In that time and place it was very difficult, if not

impossible, to change his life and the life he had been born to. It would have brought disgrace to himself and to his family. It was not really even considered as possible, so in this way it was not an option. It did not really cross his mind to try to change his profession. In many ways, he also defined himself by this work and what he did. He was very dedicated - even though it was not ideal for him- and also very skilled.' Was he married?

'He was not married, but had a child from someone he loved. This was a reason he stayed with his Master. He was bound to him as he had contracted to stay with him for a space of time and wished to stay and assist in his son's education too.' Did he ever think of himself as a killing machine and that was all he was meant to be?

'His love for his son's mother was not passionate or intense- more of a fondness. His priorities were the search for the perfect expression of the martial arts and skills-the perfect manoeuvres. It was in this way he excelled at his work. Not as a killing machine, but in the marriage of understanding of the self: power and discipline over the physical, extreme training of mind and body to work as one. Strict discipline to control his emotions, for just to allow his feelings to surge up and overwhelm him would weaken his attack and defence in a battle situation.' How old was he when he died?

'Tachaka was about 30/32 years old when he went to battle and died. His son did not become a Samurai. He grew up well and travelled away. He became a teacher and a poet, married and had seven children and his mother went to stay with them and enjoyed her grandchildren enormously. This was a happy time for all of them. The boy's mother missed him as she had both loved him and respected his strength, his discipline, his acceptance and his wisdom. Her life was not the same without him and she wished he had lived longer to be her lifetime companion. His parents looked after her and his son and became a close and loving family. They all called for his protection in their worship practice which he gave from spirit, until he reincarnated once more.'

In 2016/17, I had a most extraordinary experience during a short stay at the Hotel Conrad in East Berlin. As I was waiting in the foyer the next morning to join members of our group, I was suddenly approached by a young Japanese woman in her thirties, who became extremely excited and very red in the face when she saw me. Although I did not recognize her, she recognized me from a previous Life and immediately she asked me 'Who are you now? Where do you live?' She was accompanied a teenage girl who could not understand what the fuss was all about and gave her a questioning look. We had a brief conversation and then I left her, because the group was leaving. I wish I had asked her more questions and an address to keep in touch, but it did not occur to me. I could have tried to identify which of my many Japanese lives applied to her. Perhaps she was Tachaka's partner. I too have had similar experiences with strangers I met with briefly, but did not have the courage to speak to them [and wish I had] as she did.

Second Samurai-A Powerful Man

'Another Samurai appeared. He was about 40 years old, with a wisp of hair escaping from his helmet, in full armour, quite beautiful and heavy, he was an earlier period Samurai; good-looking. I saw a very beautiful young Japanese woman [perhaps his mother] and himself as a young child/teenager. I then saw an older Samurai, perhaps in his early 50s, in full elaborate armour, but with a different headgear, his moustache and long sparse beard turning yellowish/grey, presumably the same Samurai, a bit older and a very powerful man [Shogun[57]] controlling a large area. I felt a deep-seated pain in this man, but could not get details. I saw a battle, but then I saw a Native American Chief with long headdress, on a horse inspecting a battle' [Little Bighorn?].' [7.9.13]

87.Second Samurai-Japanese Women

Did a two-hour regression. Lot of very deeply seated pain in their lives. I could not discover the manner of death.

'I went back to the life of that Samurai in his late 40s/early 50s, in

full dark red/brown leather armour and helmet, with long, thin moustache and long, thin, pointed beard, both yellowish turning white. I saw him as a young man, perhaps early 20s, wearing a pale cream- white silk kimono with pale-blue hues, silk white socks and sandals, and long sword hanging from his waist. A rather square face with good features and beautiful black silken hair combed up. I saw him again, perhaps 10 years later, again with beautiful silk kimono and sword, and also a young woman, perhaps 18/20 years old, long, soft, hair loose on her shoulders, face with a perfect oval shape and beautiful features and eyes. I saw two or three other young beautiful women dressed in very beautiful silk kimonos, and wonderful hair. Do not know who they are. I felt I was them, but I also was the Samurai. Towards close, I saw an old man with wispy hair and long moustache and beard, dressed in dark brown simple tunic- like dress like a monk, looked like the Samurai later in his life'. [10.9.13]

Chapter 12

Revolutionary France [1789-99]

90.A Blood Relative f Louis XVI

I REGRESSED TO a life in 18th century France, at the time of the French Revolution, as an aristocrat born in Paris, living at Versailles at the Court of Louis XVI[60] very close to the King, a blood relative. I was totally unprepared for what was to follow. I stumbled upon something really bad and extraordinarily upsetting. I was sick for weeks.

'I saw a very tall athletic man by profile, with a black mark around his neck, attractive, long, wavy, chestnut-brown hair, moustache and small beard, large black piercing eyes, long face, strong manly features. He reminded me of Charles II of England. He was wearing a hat, collar, cape, knee-long boots and sword, was in his late 30s/early 40s and was surrounded by a light shadow. There was a large hall, full of light, the King's Hall, other people, and a huge archway flooded with light. I then saw him dressed in expensive black clothes and black shoes, travelling through the countryside in a carriage drawn by two horses. There is a building, rectangular in shape, dark inside with steps of stone going into a basement. He was a proud man, brought up to be proud, a good man on the wrong side of the fence. Did he agree with the King's policies? I felt his pride as he stood up, very erect, to say that he totally supported the King and wanted things to stay as they were. He felt great rage the way things turned out. Was there until the end and did not try to flee, defiant to the end. Maybe regretted not leaving Paris with the King, it should have been organized better.

He had a French wife, very young and beautiful, half his age, richly dressed, white powdery wig and white skin, beautiful peach-like complexion, who loved her husband. She paid her price for her beliefs, did not regret her beliefs, she believed in the monarchy and lived at Court with her husband. She knew things were not right outside the Palace: inequality, and, strangely, she said 'it was good it happened' and that 'it had to happen'. She was aware of the situation more than he was. They both went to the guillotine'. I always had a need to clear my throat since I was a teenager and could not wear tight necklaces [chokers]. Now I know why. For over two weeks I was very upset with great rage and maddening fury, but decided to try again and suffer this intensely traumatic experience. [16.6.14]

91.An Execution-Death by Guillotine

'Immediately I went straight into that Life and saw that aristocrat wearing a flowing white blouse, black trousers and shoes with buckles, and a dark-red scarf around his waist, in what looked like a cell full of light, but with a small window set deep into a thick wall and a desk under it, a Monsignor dressed in black with a small cape on his shoulders, a high-ranking prelate, talking to the aristocrat before the execution. I saw the man when he was a teenager, with large expressive eyes and beautiful face. I saw him travelling with others on the wooden cart, his hands tied behind his back, his feelings in turmoil, going through crowded streets, the populace shouting insults and menacing, a terrible sight!

I felt his disdain. I caught a glimpse of Marie Antoinette and the King. I saw a large crowded square and a wooden scaffold, wooden steps leading up to a block and the tall sinister shape of the guillotine.

Oh, what a sight!'

I felt his feelings, several times felt a great urge from very deep inside, rushing up from the solar plexus with great force through the chest, neck and top of the head, but it was so overpowering that I could not release it. I tried again and again without success. I felt the full impact of those feelings and was shattered, thought my chest would explode, felt very sick and nearly threw up.

'I went up the scaffold and tried again and again to catch the last thought before death, but it eluded me. I decided to go to the death scene and saw myself as this man kneeling down on the wooden block, still covered with blood from the previous execution, and placing my head on it, but still could not get the last thought. The blade went down and the head rolled down into the basket-the headless body collapsing on the other side, blood spurting out like a fountain.

What a sickening sight! And the cheering crowds!'

I was overwhelmed by a wave of compassion and great, great, maddening anger that it nearly knocked me off.

'There was a black, blank space- Death'.

Did the Soul go into the Light? I could not find out and could not continue. Extreme emotions and sickness took hold of me for weeks. I could not forget what I had seen.

Jean Pierre [Napoleon's Army]

83.Waterloo [1815] The Aftermath

This was a two-hour long regression which brought up details of three lives, the first two deeply buried under a thick wall of pain, the pain difficult to describe and to convey, and indicative of a deeply-seated trauma.

'I immediately saw a 30-year-old French Officer, Jean Pierre, a nobleman [Comte], who had joined Napoleon's army. I was wearing a French uniform, a long mantle on my shoulders and a hat like that worn by Napoleon, tall, attractive, dark, wavy hair. I saw a battlefield full of bodies; the aftermath; cannons. Terrible devastation. I saw a British Officer with epaulettes, Wellington[111] and others.' [2.9.13]

84.A Life Story

Did a two-hours regression very successfully, though could not complete it.

'I went back to the life of Jean Pierre as a beautiful little boy with blond curls; his mother, a very attractive blonde woman, very young, slender and elegant; and his father, equally elegant and good-looking, moving in the French aristocracy upper crust. Saw aristocrats at Court, dancing in a huge rectangular room, Jean Pierre as a student at the Bourbonne [?] When the Revolution[54] started he joined the rebels because he had seen the excesses of the aristocracy and resented them and later became a High-Ranking Officer in Napoleon's Army. He joined the French Army when he was 36 years old and died when he was 44 years old. He had a beautiful young wife, a brunette with deep, dark, soft eyes, very elegant'.

Death on the Battlefield

We went to his death on the battlefield. 'He was shot in the forehead and died instantly. There was no time to think, it was very quick, but he felt a huge anger at the sight of his Soldiers' bodies strewn around him and that was the feeling he carried with him in the Spirit World. He fell on them as he died, partly lying on his left side, left leg twisted open and right leg wide apart, arms bent and asunder like a ragged doll, eyes open, blood flowing from the gaping hole in the middle of his forehead.'

I ordered him to show me how he felt as he fell dying and tell me whether his Soul had left the dead body to go towards the White Light. If not, I asked him to move my toes in my left foot. Immediately, my left foot went into a spasm of contortions, as did my left leg: part of his Soul was trapped inside the body and despite the many great efforts we did, we could not release it. In the course of the regression, I went deep into this great pain and brought some of it up into the Light and released it. Did this several times until all the pain had left. It was massive and very strong and powerful, it went up my chest from deep within the solar plexus, hardly able to squeeze through my neck into the head and out through the crown chakra. It was very hard work which left me exhausted for many days and which I will have to repeat. [3.9.13]

85.Through Death's Eyes

'I saw Jean Pierre, also as a young boy and his young parents., but found it difficult to reconnect. I went to the moment of death and saw the battlefield full of bodies. Something odd happened: There was a Dark, Cloaked, Hooded, Shadow in front of me, the Grim Reaper, as we call the Angel of Death. I saw the Dark Hood and the Face/Skull inside it. The Shadow became me and I felt His presence engulfing me, my face became his Skull and my body became His body. I could feel His bones, His skeleton in place of my body. He had taken over, but I was not afraid. I went into Jean Pierre's body position when he was shot and died, reclining on the left side and asked him to leave this body because there was nothing there for him. I told him to go into the Light, and saw him as an 19th Century aristocrat, complete with long, white periwig tied back on his neck, wearing an incredibly beautiful pale-cream, pale-blue,long silk coat; silk white stockings and pale-cream silk shoes with small heels and buckles, long sword. He was looking up, young and beautiful, soft black eyes, and going up into the Light, surrounded by White Light. What a beautiful sight! I asked him to move my left hand's fingers if he had left the body, but nothing happened, so I do not know whether he went into the Light or not. Then I connected with my teenage friend and felt very upset about his early deathin this life. [5.9.13]

99. A 19thCentury Beau

So many people rushed in to come first in this regression that I was overwhelmed and found it difficult to start.

'At first, I saw a young, very elegant 19th Century man, an aristocrat, tall, slim, good-looking, with rather a longish face a bit like the actor Hugh Laurie when he was young. He had a periwig tied back with a bow, chemise with ruff at the neck and wrists, long pale-blue silk coat, cream-white breeches, white silk thighs, silk shoes with buckles, and a long decorative sword. I saw him also with a triangular hat with rolled up rim. I felt I was this man, but could not go any further.

I also saw Napoleon and his blue-coated, white breeched, generals and soldiers with rifles and bayonets; saw an old peasant woman - very chaotic.' At some point, my stomach violently contracted and something big pushed up to the throat centre, a very, very strong release, but I do not know what it is that I released.

204.A French Soldier-Waterloo[111] Another Death

I was meditating, when suddenly felt a very deep pain in my solar plexus. A Past Life slowly began to emerge.

'At first, I thought it was a German Soldier, but the very distinctive uniform, with large white strips across the chest, high, narrow hat, made me think of a French Soldier in Napoleon's Army.' Again, there is a lot of pain which has been plaguing me for months and keeping me awake at night, no matter how many Lives I access, more and more emerge. The pain is intolerable. I feel the despair of this Soldier, it is overwhelming. What happened? Who are you? I ask, but I cannot connect with him. There is a wall between us, which prevents me from accessing this Life. I cannot break through to him. I cannot rescue him. He is trapped in his own despair and will keep me awake again tonight. I am beginning to feel tired. It takes a lot of focus and I am not getting results.

'There is a pretty, young, French woman smiling at something/someone. I see a Battlefield. It is carnage. Dead horses-their legs frozen in the air, bodies, cannons, smouldering fires and wounded soldiers, all tinged in crimson, blood flowing. The aftermath of Battle. A terrible sight.'

I do not see myself. I do not see the French Soldier. I feel this extreme pain, tension, in my stomach. I am tired and want to end this unexpected regression. It is hard work, there is a lot of resistance. 'I see this Soldier, with bayonet and rucksack on his back, deafening noise, trumpets, screams, firing ammunitions, explosions, Hell broken loose. It is a lot to take in, to witness. I do not see the Soldier.' I am tired and end the session. [4.4.19]

Chapter 13

Wild Bill [Bill Hickok 1837-76]

99.Regrets

I VISITED DEADWOOD, South Dakota, in 2015, and no. 10 Saloon where Bill Hickok was killed and where a strong presence remained which I took back home with me, totally unaware of this. 'Amazingly, Wild Bill[65]came in, tall, slim, good- looking, with cowboy hat, longish hair and face, moustache, wearing a long coat, belt, and of course, a gun. I saw him very close up, quite young perhaps late 20s early 30s. Saw a gold-rush town, Deadwood, the main street.' I could not get rid of Bill. I asked him if he had any regrets and a thought came to me: 'A family'.

Watching Over Me

'Wild Bill' is stooping over me now as I write. I suddenly thought he wants to protect me. Thank you, Bill! He is laughing.' He would not go away. I told him I was in the middle of a regression, and even got up to get a glass of water, but he was still there when I came back and is here behind me as I write this. He is very persistent. I sent him towards the White Light and he disappeared into it for a while, but then came back and is still here as I write. I drew a curtain over him and continued with the regression. [19.5.15]

117.Stuck by Me-A Lasting Presence

This was part of a complex Regression with many Lives.

'Wild Bill' suddenly appeared and I could not send him away, although I tried hard. He is behind me as I write, very protective. Told him not to drop in when I am doing a regression, but it is too late to stop him now.

Chapter 14

Native American Lives 19th Century]

4.Scenes of Indian Life

'I SEE AN Indian encampment, a man wearing heavy clothes [animal skin]; behind him trees, deep green, beautiful fir trees, very tall, deep green trees; mountains with white tops in the background. It is an encampment in a valley, a very peaceful valley, beautiful blue sky. Another Indian is holding a spear, his hair neatly divided in two tresses, with feathers at the back of the head; wearing a jacket; a Chief with a beautiful headdress of feathers, heavy jacket, with an interesting face, not a young man, sitting with his legs crossed, quietly smoking a pipe.

There is an enclosure, a tepee, they are all sitting in a circle, naked to the waist; a fire in the middle of the circle, soft light on the faces of the people sitting around it, a very peaceful setting. A man is wearing a bison's skull from which a mantle falls from the top of his head down on his shoulders. He is naked to the waist under the mantle, wearing arm bracelets, smoking a pipe, looking into the fire very thoughtfully. Two or three young beautiful men, also naked to the waist and feathers on the back of their heads, with long spears, are looking towards me and beyond me.

There is a prairie, bison, huge, beautiful animals like living sculptures, grazing peacefully in this valley, majestic bodies very, very beautiful, and a feeling of unbounded freedom which fills the Soul.

A Hunt

An Indian man wearing a feather necklace, bracelets on his arms and on his wrists, very good-looking, holding a tomahawk in one hand and a spear in the other, looks in my direction, but not at me, further in the distance. Suddenly, I see bison fleeing, running wildly, and he is watching the direction in which they run. [15.12.92]

A Tragic Death

An Indian man has been run over, stampeded upon by bison running away at great speed and is fast disappearing under their feet, his arms raised backward. I am not sure whether he is the same Indian I just saw. I just see this man, I see this man, I cannot see his arms, he is thrown backwards as he quickly disappears under the bison's feet. Later, Crazy Horse told me I had a great Spiritual experience at the beginning of that Life, but I only saw the end of it.

An Assassin

I see this Indian wearing a full headdress of feathers, a Chief, looking out into the distance under the blue sky, bison in the valley moving gently, peacefully and slowly as they graze. I see an Indian wearing a cape, a full headdress of feathers, standing on a rock overlooking the scenery, looking down on the landscape surrounding him, scanning the distance with his eyes like an eagle as if he is looking for something. Another Indian man stands behind him, naked, strange, not very good-looking, with a lance/spear behind the Chief and he is stabbing the Chief in the back-the scene is not clear-not sure. I see a Chief--not the same person-laid out on a bed inside a tepee, dead; another Indian with him, half naked to the waist, a feather on the back of his head-not sure what is going on, not sure what he is doing-various scenes superimposing on one another. An old man, his face all lined, his hair neatly combed in one single tress at the back of his head, lost in thoughts.

A Family

I see the face of a young woman[1], her hair neatly combed back- not sure what she is doing-good face, in her 20s or early 30s, hair dark ash-blonde, not brown, lovely face, soft brown eyes, well-shaped mouth, soft colour on her cheeks and lips, wearing an apron, pounding something [food]. On her left-hand side, there is an old Indian man, actually not so old, looking very strong, in his late 40s or early 50s. I am confused now. This man in front of me, a feather at the back of his head, not dark skinned, dressed like an Indian, looking like an Indian, his hair is dark, but not so dark. I see an Indian man again, fir trees in the background, blue sky, some Indian women in the distance. One is inside a tepee, she is wearing long dress and trousers, her hair loose on her shoulders, lovely features, she is not dark skinned, although she has lovely black eyes, soft black eyes, not dark skinned, very long hair falling neatly on her back and shoulders, very young-do not know what she is doing, seems to be looking at something.

Misgivings

See an older man on the right-hand side of this picture. Again, a Chief with full headdress of feathers, about 50 years old, with lined face, see him by profile, smoking a pipe and staring in front of him lost in his thoughts. Again, a circle of Indian men inside a tepee, naked to the waist and this man with the bison's skull and horns on his head, not sure what is going on, quite a few people in the tepee, legs crossed in front of them, this young man with a good face, wearing feathers of different shapes on his head. See another Indian, a younger man, his skin not dark, blue eyes. Another Indian in the distance now, a very good face, older, dark skinned, this Indian, beautiful young man in his early 30s-not sure what is going on, rocks in the background, the light is falling. A white man, an Indian with him-not sure what is going on, this Chief with a full headdress of feathers, light is falling, the ground is very powdery-not sure what they are doing. I see a man, a good face, his hair parted in the middle of his forehead, one feather on the back of his head, his hair falling gently on the sides of his face, neatly arranged in a tress at the back, good features, wearing a cape on top of his jacket staring in front of him- not sure what is going on. Another Indian, younger, very beautiful, hair loose on his shoulders, half naked to the waist, necklace, bracelets, in very good shape. Again, I see the Indian Chief, very impressive, he is a young man, looking into the distance, I can see the mountains.' [2.11.1996]

6.The Home Coming

'My Indian Friends are all here with me today. They are all gathered here, there seem to be so many of them. I see those close to me very well, and the other ones are a bit in the shadow, all gathered here today, they have all come here and are looking at me. There are many. I can see some well, beautiful headdresses of feathers with white and blue tips and the sky is blue, the sky is blue, but it looks as if it is getting dark and my people are here all gathered around me. I am an Indian man wearing a full head of feathers and sitting quietly on the ground, my feet crossed in front of me, my arms falling gently on the side of my body and my hands folded like cups on the side of my ankles, am sitting very erect. Another Indian man is opposite me sitting like me, with black hair, in his forties, just sitting opposite me, with an aquiline nose and a rather long, narrow face with close-set eyes. He is wearing a band on his head and he is sitting opposite me.

Another Indian on the left-hand side is sitting like us, inside a tepee. There is another Indian on my right-hand side and we are sitting at the four points of the Cross, one, two, three, four points of the Cross. I see another Indian now, beautiful face, he has a white feather at the back of his head and is dressed in white, has rather a bony face, possibly in his forties, early fifties. He is sitting right opposite me and is looking at me straight into my eyes, he has very nice features, even looks a bit Japanese, but he is not, he is Indian.

I am sitting very erect with all my feathers, a full crown of feathers on my head. There is an old Chief opposite me and he looks very authoritative. He has a bundle of feathers on the back of his head and is wearing a fur mantle. He looks very important and is staring ahead of himself and now is looking down at me, his eyes are very red, beautiful eyes, looking at me very seriously. His features are very strong, beautiful. He is looking at me very seriously, staring at me, very thoughtful, deep penetrating look, very beautiful mouth and nose, very good strong features. Very thoughtful, there is a Light behind him. There is another Indian. They seem to be wearing ceremonial clothes. They are all gathered in front of me. I am walking amongst them, and they open up creating a space and I walk between them. I am wearing my ceremonial robes. I am wearing my full head of feathers. There is a very tall Indian man, he enters the tepee and I go inside with him. There is a small circle of Indian Chiefs gathered around a fire, smoking their pipes, and I sit amongst them. They look serious, they are not talking, they are staring at me, and the oldest Chief takes the pipe from his mouth and passes it on to me and I smoke a few puffs and hand it all around so that the others can join us. I am overwhelmed with emotion.

More Indians enter the tepee and are joining the circle around us, they have come to greet me, women and children. They take me by the hand outside the tepee into the encampment and there is a man with two white feathers on the back of his head. I see his profile, he is staring in front of him, his eyes sad, he is opposite me now, his hair is parted in the middle and falling gently on the sides of his face, gathered in one tress on the back. The encampment is very peaceful, there is great peace. It is daylight, people are coming out of their lodges to see me, the women with their children, young and old. I feel emotional, I cry again for joy at seeing them again. They all come up to me. I am standing very tall. I can see myself now. I am very tall, well built. I have a very strong face, I have a few feathers on the back of my head, am not wearing my full headdress now, I am staring in front of myself, am very thoughtful. I have a very strong Indian face, I do not know what tribe we are, the name has not been given to me, quite an oval face, the skin is olive colour and the hair is very black, soft and beautiful, am very tall and very well built, standing with my legs open [apart] and my hands folded on my chest.

At Peace with Nature and the Soul

I am overlooking the Plain, a vast valley, a huge valley with some rocks and canyons in the background, a huge valley, and the sun is high in the sky and all is peace and all is beauty and serenity in Nature and in our hearts. I stare in front of me, enjoying the space and the vastness, the quietude, the blue skies and the sun high in the sky and the bison grazing gently, undisturbed. It is a moment of great peace and beauty. I feel at one with Creation, with this world which belongs to me. I feel at one with this world. I stare in front of myself for a very long time. There is a feeling of freedom, of unbounded freedom, freedom in the heart, freedom in the mind, freedom in the body and around me, unbounded spaces of great beauty which reveal the hand of God. I am so grateful to be given this opportunity to be back with my People. I take a deep breath, what a beautiful face. I see myself now, what a very manly face, chiselled nose, high cheek bones, very well shaped mouth and eyebrows, black eyes.

Saying Goodbye

The scene is now changing and I do not know what is happening now. I am back at the encampment. There is heaviness in my heart. I see people again around me, the light is falling, it is getting darker. I see their backs against the light staring at me silently. They look sad. They look sad. I am not wearing any ornaments. An Indian man is staring at me steadily, and I look at them all, there is great silence, no word is spoken. My hair is falling gently on one side of my face, very softly, combed into a tress. I am wearing a jacket, trousers. I am very tall, there is sadness in my heart. It is a parting again. There is sadness in my heart, where there was joy now there is sorrow.

Through Death into the White Light

We are facing one another for a long time, silently. Someone is approaching me, carrying something in his hands, on his arms. My heart centre is wide open. I cannot see properly. I have been given something. I do not know what it is. My heart chakra is wide open. I appear to be raising myself above ground. I see the people from high above. I am lifted higher and higher above and they remain below and are looking up at me. I am higher and higher up in the sky and they are below, below, yes, they are disappearing from my sight, from high up in the sky. I am covered in a cloud of White Light and my People have gone. I do not see them anymore. They have gone. I see myself in a cloud of White Light high up in the sky. I have something in my arms. I do not know what it is. I have a smile on my face and I am now dressed in white, all in white, a full headdress of feathers and at the same time I seem to wear a band around my head, and my black hair is softly falling on my shoulders. I am carrying something but do not know what it is.

A Boundless Sea of White Emptiness

Again, I am sitting on the ground very erect with legs crossed, my arms falling gently on my lap, hands open gently like a cup, sitting and staring ahead at something, but do not see anything except spaces, white spaces, vast spaces, white, white clouds, and am looking sad in front of me, very thoughtful. I seem an older man, sadness in my face, sadness in my heart. I am very thoughtful, very thoughtful. I am staring in front of me and my head is full of thoughts, and I am by myself. My heart chakra is very open again. I do not know where I am, there does not seem to be anything around, only empty spaces, only white empty spaces. I am wearing a full head of feathers now and am by myself and am sad. I think of all my loved ones, those I left behind. My heart yearns for them.

There is an old man, an old man, it is the same man but older, his face is thinner, the features seem to have drawn closer, it is the face of the man with the aquiline nose and the rather narrow long oval face, I feel as if I am that man. I do not know how old that man is, he seems to be unwell, sitting with crossed legs but bending over in front of him. I do not know what is happening now. Out of that weak old man a younger, stronger, more beautiful, powerful man has risen from the ground. Oh, he is beautiful and is standing up on his feet, very tall, very strong, very powerful, naked to the waist, he is not black, his skin is white, beautiful face. Oh, I do not know what this is. He is standing very tall and erect with his arms across his chest and looks the image of strength and power and health. There is the encampment, the blue sky, and there are the trees, fir trees, on the left-hand side, and it all looks so beautiful - this encampment and the blue sky and in the distance the white peaks they look so beautiful and peaceful, horses grazing the grass. What a lovely encampment. The sky is very blue, just a few white clouds, beautiful.

I am standing under a tree overlooking the encampment and think how much I love my home, how much I love my people, and yet I must go, and yet I must leave them. I am under a huge tree and its branches are spread all over and they cover me like a huge umbrella and I feel the love coming from that tree deep down into my being, into my very soul. I feel that tree is part of myself and I carry all the love and all the knowledge of my People in myself, deep, deep down, the very essence of my being. I carry it with me into my very soul, into my very soul, into my very soul. I wish I did not have to leave. I wish I did not have to go. I wish I could stay here for ever.

The Summoning

I see the shape of a Roman Soldier brandishing his sword, he has a brick-red mantle falling from his shoulder. I do not see him very well. I see him against the sky. It is time to go, it is time to go. Yes. I see the Soldier, a Roman General, he has come to tell me I must go and I do not want to go. But he is brandishing a Sword of Light towards me and I know I must go. I wish I could take something back with me.

An old Indian, the bony, heavily lined face, dressed in white, is looking at me, holds a stick in his hands. He is looking at me. He is giving me my headdress of feathers and I hold it in my hands, against my heart, against my chest. I am overwhelmed with emotion, with joy. This Indian is again in front of me, looking at me. I ask him to let me carry the feathers with me. I see the old Chief, the bony little face wearing a full headdress of feathers touching the ground, he is looking at me, he is not very tall, he is old, standing very erect and is looking at me. I see him again - he has no full headdress of feathers now, only one. I am going back now, I am going back, and I am feeling cold, I am feeling cold as I sit back in my chair.

Death

I see the old Chief laying down, with his full head of feathers around him, he is laid out. I see his body. He is dead and I am that body. I am dressed all in white and wearing a full headdress of white feathers, my jacket is white, pure white, resplendent white, my trousers are white, resplendent white, my moccasins are white, resplendent white, and I take my feathers with me. I am feeling full of Light, there is a lot of White Light around me, I am wearing all my white feathers and am standing very erect dressed all in white and there is a lot of Light all around me, pure White and Yellow Light. This Light radiates from me and is very powerful, very powerful.

My body is cold, the Light is all around me, I am bathed in Light, in all Light, Golden Light and White Light. I am standing very erect and my face is raised towards Heaven where this Light is coming from. I am blessed into this Light. It washes from me all traces of Darkness, it purifies my Soul and I am born again, a new Soul, a new Spirit. I am born again. I am a new Spirit, a new Soul, all traces of Darkness have been washed away.

I have come home. I am buried in my father's Indian village. Love governs us all and all the skies and all the cosmic oceans.' [11.4.1993]

7.Scenes of Indian Life

Two Past Lives in this regression.

'I see an Indian man in his 40s, naked to the waist, a feather on the back of his head, trees to the left and to the right, blue sky, tepees, horses grazing; a quiet life close to nature, a few scattered clouds like cotton wool. I see another Indian in his 30s, beautiful and fit and then an older Indian in his 60s/70s. There is a feeling of peace, close to Nature. Mountains in the background covered with snow, a valley where the tepees are. Indian man with a crib in front of him, bending over the crib, a child in his arms, putting the child into the crib, a big nose but a kind look in his eyes, looks very intently at the child in the crib horses on one side, crib out in open air, sky beautiful, crib resting on green grass-has taken the child out of the crib into his arms.

A very beautiful Indian woman, beautiful black eyes, very soft, the most beautiful face I ever saw. Behind her another Indian man with beautiful Light behind him which puts him in the shadow. Jesus comes through.

There is a village in the background-a Catholic Nun appears-a glimpse of the Indian woman [carrying a child on her back?]. A little Indian child [2/3 years old] a little feather behind his head, naked to the waist, fat little arms, lovely little face, beautiful soft eyes, on his father's back. He looks very happy, a lovely soft light in its eyes; the child looks very happy, skin quite light, tiny little teeth, soft little smile, rather longish face but beautiful, very fine, light-black hair, beautiful round soft eyes, little nose, very beautiful features, lovely child, skin looks quite white.

A Premonition

Older Indian in his 60s looks enigmatic, he was the younger man mentioned, the face is the same, with very few lines, very good features, very sculptured features. Superimposed on him, the face of Jesus with the Cross, with the Crown of Thorns, a short beard and a moustache, pale light-brown hair, very good nose, very good features, standing by the Cross fully clothed, like a cloak, in the distance the Indian village, now wearing a proper Crown. I see the trees on one side, dark green.

An adolescent child, 12 years old or so, not seen clearly, an Indian man, very good features, quite a dark skin. An Indian camp; a woman and a man in his forties under a tree, the man embracing the woman who seems to be crying. A tepee with the body of a Big Chief laid out wearing a beautiful crown of feathers, his hands crossed on the stomach; someone with him looking down at him, a young person, in the light, a woman in her 20s, very beautiful skin, soft eyes, with a fringed jacket and a feather in her hair; her skin is not dark, beautiful face [the child at the beginning, there is a resemblance] must be cold, she is wearing a heavy jacket.

I feel as if I am an Indian man, the Indian bending over the crib, it is darker, the light has fallen and there is a gentle peace. Inside his tepee a very suffused light, the Indian man dressed in white, with beautiful features, another man with him, some people under the moonlight, this lovely man, this beautiful face, very soft face. Indian man with young adolescent boy and young girl on each side, his children, about 14/15 years old, walking, going somewhere; beautiful tall trees; a family group; strange people dressed in black, brandishing something; Indian his hands crossed on his chest.'

36.Native American Burial

'I saw a dead Chief in a Valley on top of a wooden platform, and a broken spear with many beautiful feathers at the foot of a wooden bed covered by a large animal skin. On the bed a body in ceremonial clothes wearing a long crown of feathers, bone jewellery on the chest. In the background, a deep orange-red, blood-stained sky and the sun fast disappearing under the horizon.' [20.3.2000]

39.Wounded Knee[16] [1890]

'I felt getting older-an old Indian Chief-and saw myself about 40/50 years old and then growing older and physically heavier. I was sitting and was this old man, now very old and with a very lined face, looking back on his life.

I saw an Indian village, tepees, horses, trees, valleys. I felt great heaviness and pain in the heart. I entered a tepee and it was all very dark. At first, an old man lay dead on a bed.

I moved backward and forward in that Life. I saw a young woman with a boy [6 or 7 years old]. Then a massacre[16] in a field or a valley: many Indians dead. I saw a dark-blue cloud and in it a cavalry of soldiers, sabres shining in the sunlight, in dark-blue uniforms, and rifles, horses galloping away.' I moved forward in that Life and saw the tepee again. I felt great oppression and pain in the throat and heart chakra, very uncomfortable. My Mother [my Helper] was always with me from the beginning to the end of the regression. I asked her that I be shown what was inside the tepee that gave me such extreme pain. I entered the tepee it was very dark. I imagined it full of light, but still did not see anything. I moved backward and forward in that Life and again and again ended up with the tepee and could not see what was inside it. [8.3.2009]

54.Black Hills-South Dakota USA

I did a shamanic journey with the drum and immediately was back to the Black Hills. 'I saw an Indian lady. I saw an Indian man and felt I was him, one feather at the back of the head, open leather waistcoat on naked chest, cotton trousers. Saw a village by the trees, the Black Hills. I saw it covered with snow and so were the trees. People wearing heavy winter clothes, woollen shawls. I was one of them. Lovely scene of Indian village life. Glad I was part of it.' [25.6.13]

77.Old Chief's Death-Black Hills

'I saw an Indian settlement by a wood [the Black Hills], tepees, men wearing what looked like blankets over their shoulders [winter?], but the trees were covered with leaves. Tepees against the dark-blue, moonless sky and the trees. I entered one and sat against a bright fire with others. Saw various Indian men, some young some old, an old Chief, dead, and later, another Chief, small face and features, very old, wearing a long headdress, and heavy clothes, beautiful'. I do not know how the old Chief was when he died, but I think he died a natural death, although I felt a deep-seated pain when I saw him. [10.8.13]

93.An Apparition

'I first saw Jesus with long blond hair and wearing a very light-pink tunic with a waist belt. I then saw Death on a white horse charging full speed towards me, brandishing a sword and stopping right in front of me, his Skull with a very hostile, savage, expression, jaws open, the Sword in the air ready to strike. I did not budge and stood my ground, staring the Skull into the empty eye- sockets and was not afraid. He looked at me angrily, with rage, and then, somehow, disappeared'.

Preparing to Fight

'I then went to the Black Hills, to an Indian village. Saw an old Chief [possibly in his 50s] with a beautiful headdress of feathers [full length], ceremonial dress. I saw his face very clearly and then I saw him as a younger man [early 30s] with one feather at the back of his head, naked to the waist, good-looking, carrying a bow. Then something extraordinary happened. I saw a fire at night and Indian men dancing around it, all with buffalo horns on their heads, naked to the waist, perhaps in preparation for a hunt. Suddenly, I saw a buffalo in front of me, his face opposite mine, his eyes looking straight into mine and I felt my face and body turning into that buffalo, strong neck, shoulders and body. I felt the power, the strength of this animal coming into my body. I was him for some time. Then out of the buffalo came an Indian man with a buffalo's head on his head and they were one, and he rode this buffalo on the plains. I then saw a wolf staring at me, his face very close to mine, and again I became that wolf and felt his strength and power, and again saw an Indian man with a wolf's head on his head. Finally, a big, brown bear was facing me, staring into my eyes and again I became that bear and felt his strength and power'. [20.10.14]

94.Little Bighorn [1876]

A three-hour long regression which brought up a lot of stuff and emotions. 'I saw an Indian Village in the Black Hills, with a forest behind and a large open space in the front, a man with buffalo horns on his head, naked to the waist, and others around a big fire with big flames casting lights and shadows on their faces. I also saw another Indian in full gear, with a beautiful long feather headdress and clothes. I was these men. I saw buffaloes in flight, and then again grazing peacefully in the prairie.

An Ominous Sight: Custer

I saw US cavalry men and an Officer [Custer] many times over and very close up, saw his face very clearly, short blondish hair and moustache, not seen much under his hat, and short beard, small pointed face under the brim of his hat. I saw Jesus and felt I was Jesus looking down the Cross. Saw the Indian village again and myself as a young, tall, good-looking Indian man, one feather at the back of the head, my hair combed neatly with a loop behind my head, naked to the waist, with a beautiful bone necklace and pectoral. Saw a beautiful young Indian woman, perhaps his wife, and a few old Indian men. Saw buffaloes again, one very close, looking into my eyes, feeling myself turning into him again, my face his face, his energy my energy.

Saw the same officer charging a cavalry army and descending like an ominous black cloud into the prairies, going down a ravine with his horse, Indians on horses galloping towards them, brandishing axes, tomahawks, charging at great speed, clashing, in full direct combat, man to man, many dead, the officer riding through the devastated village, tepees destroyed, burnt out fires. Little Bighorn[62] came to mind [1876], and also Wounded Knee. I saw a dead Indian laid out inside a tepee [a young man perhaps 30/35 years old].' I could not get his last thought or know whether his Soul went into the Light, though I felt it might have done so unbroken, in its full entirety. 'I also saw an older man with one feather back on his head [perhaps myself] staring at the dead man, right in front of him, lost in his thoughts.' [26.10.14]

95.Wounded Knee

I went back to the Black Hills and saw the Indian Village by the trees and became an Indian Chief again, sitting, with a long feather headdress.' He is now writing this account and I feel extreme pain in the solar plexus and great sorrow in the chest. I went deeply into this Life, but I did not get a full picture.

Genocide

'I saw bits and pieces, including Custer, crowds of Indian women and children running away in panic; then US cavalry descending from a hill clashing with Indians.

Then I saw Nefertiti briefly. This is the second time she came to me in the last few days.' [27.10.14]

I shall not rest quiet
in Montparnasse
you may bury my body
in Sussex grass
you may bury my tongue
in Champmedy
I shall not be there
I shall rise and pass
bury my heart
at Wounded Knee
Stephen Vincent Benet

107.A Glimpse - Custer

'I saw a US Cavalry and General Custer very clearly.' Something released from my throat. [30.5.15]

114.Sitting Bull

'I was a very old Indian man possibly in my 70s, or at least he looked old to me. At first, was not sure whether I was a man or a woman, with a sort of pear-shaped face, hooked nose, strong features, heavy lined, not unpleasant. Sitting Bull. [88] I went back a few years and saw a young Indian man in his early 30s and then the same strong-faced Indian man in his late 30s wearing a headdress with a bull's horns.

Little Big Horn [1876]

Saw Indian warriors on horses galloping at great speed, charging, their spears pointing forward, led by the man with the bull's horns on his head, perhaps a buffalo hunt, but did not see any buffaloes.

Saw a Confederate soldier, perhaps a general, in typical blue uniform, large hat, big moustache, dark- blond hair, square face, in his late 30s, not Custer, do not know who he is, did not get further details.

Saw the Black Hills[89] and an old Indian woman lost in thoughts. Saw the Black Hills again, and felt a heavy pain in my stomach, deeply seated, very heavy, filling up my chest, deep pain. A thought crossed my mind:

A Jewel we lost.' [7.6.15]

115.On the Attack-Custer

'Immediately I started the regression I saw the pear- faced Indian man and he became me. I wasoverwhelmed by a feeling of extreme bitterness.

I saw Indian warriors on horses, their long spears pointing forward, a battle. Saw Custer very clearly, blue uniform, hat, sword, going down a ravine. I saw a village backing on woods, saw the Great Plains, enormous feeling of freedom: All lost!' [8.6.15]

116.Regrets

Did one-hour regression. As soon as I started, Sitting Bull appeared and became me.

'Saw the Black Hills and I was a young Sitting Bull and then older. Could not get the last thought before being shot. I tried my best for my people at the Pine Ridge Reservation, but that was not enough. Extreme feeling of sadness.'

I felt very tired and had to lie down for half an hour or so, still in the regression. I got up, Sitting Bull still with me, overwhelmed by a feeling of powerlessness, impotence, unable to revert the tide of things, despair filling my chest, heavy, heavy on my heart.

'What we had and what we lost!

Shot in the back by one of my people! Betrayal!'
flashed through the mind. [9.6.15]

137.Indian Chief-White Man's Greed

I felt very agitated and started a regression to discover what it was.

'Slowly, an Indian man, long trousers, moccasins, naked to the waist, one feather at the back of his head, possibly in his early 30s, materialises in my chair and I disappear into that Past Life.' I feel a very strong pain in the solar plexus, almost unbearable.

'A military man, of high rank, dark-blue uniform, medals, blond hair parted on one side, moustache, not Custer, I think, appears. Perhaps it is Custer, not sure.

I see the Plains in all their glory. Now I am a Chief, with long feather headdress, short tunic, long sleeves and trousers. I am old, my face is heavily lined. I feel tension in my heart, stomach-ache.

'In my long life, I witnessed the destruction of my People, of our way of life. We succumbed to the White Man's greed. All our Tears could not wash away our Sorrow.

A Bitter Death

I am inside my tepee, in front of a small fire, squatting on the ground, blanket on my shoulders, smoking a small pipe, my life all spent, no joy, many dead, ghosts of a recent past. They are here, waiting for me. Images of happier times flick in front of me. I sink deep into my body. That is how they find me in the morning.' I cry.

141.The Power of Deceit

Just back from the Black Hills. I am sure I brought someone back with me.

'I see the Black Hills, I am a Chief, with a long feather headdress which touches the ground. I am wearing a long tunic, trousers and moccasins.' I feel my face changing.

'I am Sitting Bull, with strong face and features.

I see the buffaloes roaming freely in the Plains.

I have a heavy heart and tears are raining down my face. The appearance of the White Man on our lands spelt disaster for our People. We knew we would lose them and our way of life would be destroyed, but we believed in false promises.' I feel great heaviness in the solar plexus area, mixed with pain.

'I am now wearing a long breastplate and buffalo horns on my head. I am the Spiritual Leader of my People and a Healer, but could not heal their greatest affliction, White Man.' I feel a wave of bitterness coming over me.

'A traitor and a coward struck me in the back, the only way he could do it!' I feel disgust and pain, as my stomach twists around and around, and great heaviness and pain in the heart area. 'I see an Indian man, perhaps in his late 40s, with a good face and good features, heavy lined, masses of black hair tied back and a single feather, long breastplate and tunic, sad and thoughtful.' I have stomach-ache, feel sick. The sickness intensifies. [9.9.15]

183.Through Death into A Native American Life

I have been feeling restless and upset for the last few weeks, so it is time to do a regression to find out what it is that troubles me. I cannot ignore these symptoms for long, they simply will not be ignored and demand attention. I am beginning to feel a deep pain in my solar plexus [stomach], something is stirring up from the depth of my soul. I do not know what it is, but it is beginning to upset me, deep, deep, down. And now the pain is there, like a black monster, and I take it head on. It is very intense. I wonder what it is all about. I dive into it. Feel the pain and let go. I struggle under its weight. This Past Life is very resistant, does not want to reveal itself and my whole heart chakra is affected and I rock to and fro in my chair, like a cradle, in great pain.

'I went through a black, black Mass and stepped out of the Confines of Life into the Confines of Death to retrieve this Life which so affects me still. I am not afraid. I have died so many times that Death is a good Friend to me. I ask for His help, and He guides me through this Journey. I feel safe and protected. Suddenly, my Mother appears, to reassure me. All is well. My maternal Grandfather also appears. I am beyond physical pain, now. He is here in front of me. I am totally relaxed.

There is a Native American in front of me, I am that Indian. I am beginning to feel tired now. This man is not old, perhaps 40, I cannot tell his age. What is behind this Life?' It is like peeling an onion. [11.1.18]

Chapter 15

Tudor England
Catherine Parr [1512-1548]-Henry VIII
Queen Consort [1543-47]

34.A Happy Couple-A Good Wife

THIS REGRESSION MADE me very sad, full of unfulfilled promise. 'I saw Anne Boleyn[11], and then Henry VIII[13]

I was Catherine Parr[12] Henry bent over to me and whispered in my ear 'I miss you, Kate'[12] He still thinks fondly of me, because I helped him reduce his pain levels and visits me because he still cares for me. Henry and I were happy together. I talked to him and listened to him and comforted him about his future. I helped him bring back his faith in the future and trust in the Universal Spiritual Life, although we often argued on religious issues. I persuaded him to restore his family and, in this way, I helped Anne Boleyn's daughter[14].

I knew Anne Boleyn very well and briefly experienced life through her by sharing words and ideas with her. I discussed religion with her, and later her daughter lived with me. Anne was a few years older than me and she was someone I admired. I never knew I would one day take the same husband as she had had. Sadly, I died trying to bear a child. This was the husband I took after Henry. This man[15] did not make me as happy as he had promised me.

Henry VIII was a complex, multi-faceted man. He could be humorous, gentle, supportive, but then could switch to being ruthless, self-obsessed and feeling hard- done by-suffering for his people, and so on. I was a good wife to him, but he was not an ideal husband for me. As Catherine, my personality was similar to me today. My death was sad as it was inadequate care which meant I became ill and died of the fever.'

57.An Untimely Death

This Life is another source of pain and disquiet. I did an hour-long regression and went straight into Catherine Parr's life, the very last moments. I asked her what were her feelings before death? The answer was as sharp as a blade cutting through the flesh: 'Pain, loneliness, despair, frustration, betrayal.' It took my breath away. I was devastated and sick for days. The memory of that pain would not go away.

'I saw her husband, Thomas Seymour.'[36] [8.7.13]

83.16th Century Man [Thomas Seymour?]

'I saw a rich nobleman, young and good-looking, perhaps in his early 30s, with a thin moustache and short, dark, thick beard [perhaps Thomas Seymour, Catherine Parr's husband], wearing a hat [more like a beret] and a short, very beautiful coat like those of Henry VIII, of that period. Could not get more detail. I saw Henry VIII.'

85.An Older Henry VIII

Henry VIII also dropped in, with a short beard-never seen him like that before, later in his life as an older man.

102.Visions

'I entered a portal opening on pale-grey clouds, went into them and saw myself very young and beautiful with an inner light, dark-blonde hair with a reddish hue, wavy and shoulder-length, parted in the middle, [Catherine Parr?], wearing a pale-grey tunic. I walked into the clouds floating past me. I sat down and waited and started walking again. The sky was full of greyish clouds. I wondered whether I was in Limbo, a state between states. I stopped and started the meditation again to see if there were changes, but it was exactly the same. I asked for help and guidance from Mary. She came to me as the Virgin Mary of Medjugorje in Bosnia, exactly like that, beautiful. I saw a Catholic Nun with roses[71][a Saint] another Nun, then Padre Pio[7] during Mass giving me Communion, and he was with me for some time.

120.Young Henry VIII [1491-1547]

Yesterday I did a regression but could not continue as too many lives came up at once and could not select one, they all wanted to be first. I felt a strong pain in the stomach, but could not get details. This morning I woke up feeling upset and all trembling inside, very strong pain in the solar plexus, so I decided to investigate this and started the regression immediately.

'I was wearing an armour, visor down, jousting. I saw a 16th Century man with a rather rectangular face, good- looking, perhaps 30 years old, wavy blond hair, moustache and chin beard [Henry VIII]. Out of the mist came Anne Boleyn, Jane Seymour, a [Spanish?] cardinal, James I, and others. It was like sifting through scattered, mixed, archive papers' [13.6.15]

142.Elizabeth I [1533-1603]-An Unhappy Life?

'Elizabeth I[102] appeared in full regalia as she was on her coronation day. I then saw her as she was much later in her life, still with her crown and jewels, but an older woman. I saw her again as a young girl on her coronation and also in stages in between, as a young woman. In the first, it looked as if her crown was too big and heavy for her small head, and so did the rich clothes for her waif- like body, as if she was a bit overwhelmed by it all. I see Elizabeth as she appeared in a portrait as an old woman, with crown, jewels, and a darker red sumptuous dress, with gown large at the side as was the fashion, a gaunt face, eyes large and feverish in their gaze:

An unhappy woman?'

I finished the regression because too many lives from various historical periods came in, all wanting to be seen first. [17.9.15]

185.A Tormented Soul

As I felt the usual physical/mental discomfort I decided to do another regression.

'I immediately saw the bust of a 12/14-year-old girl, her reddish hair neatly combed back revealing a tall forehead, a very pretty face and lively, intelligent, eyes. I saw another girl/woman, unsure who she was, then the young girl again. I then saw Catherine Parr, a lovely, slim, young woman. I was overwhelmed by a feeling of pain, disappointment, unhappiness. She is not at peace.' I feel pain in my stomach. I became her as I sit and write this.

Henry VIII's True Love

'I am wearing an expensive dark-red dress with long, bell-shaped sleeves. I am rich. My husbands provided me with all the necessities of life and comforts, though they did not love me and I did not love them, they were too old, but I was a good wife. I was not unhappy and accepted the standards of that time. I was lucky, many women were not. I had everything I needed and more. Henry did love me truly in his own way. He was happy with me, although he liked to be in control of people and situations, always. He was a control freak, always suspicious of everything and jealous of his power over people and land. He was a very difficult man to live with, but he truly loved me.' [15.1.18]

201.Young Henry-Catherine/Charlotte Parallel Lives

'I was meditating, when I suddenly saw a 16th century man, at the time of Henry VIII, very well dressed, with a kind of triangular hat, light-red beard and moustache, early 30s. I did not recognise him at first, then it was Henry himself as I never saw him before, young and good-looking. I was not trying to do a regression, so I was surprised. I became very heavy and knew I was sliding back into the Past. I saw Catherine Parr, young and beautiful, with a very soft face and eyes. I became her. There is still so much of Catherine in me, she is one of my most enduring incarnations with her enthusiasm for life and resourceful nature, compassionate heart and naivete. I see Charlotte Bronte, two parallel Lives, two unhappy women.' [26.3.19]

17th Century England

85.Charles I [r. 1625-1649]-An Appearance

Did two-hour regression and tried to connect to Jean Pierre, but with some difficulty, because other people dropped in. Charles I[55] came in very vividly but I had to ask him to leave, because I was in the middle of a Soul Rescue in a Past Life. He is here with me as I write this, with white lace embroidered collar, long curly hair, distinctive nose and large intelligent eyes. I promised him I would go back to him next regression

18th-19th Century England

121.Nelson [1758-1805] Battle at Sea

Did one-hour regression. Two or three lives came in, not much detail, a bit chaotic.

'I was an Admiral[98] in the British Navy, 18th century. I saw a beautiful ship with beautiful white sails, striking, gliding fast across the sea. I was wearing a triangular hat with white rolled up rims, a long pale-blue coat on a long waistcoat with a scarf across the chest, breeches, stockings and shoes with buckles, wearing a periwig, tied behind, and two curls of hair on each side of the face. I was a young man with blond hair. Saw abattle at sea, two ships encroaching on one another[99].

Nelson-Jean Pierre-Parallel Lives

Then I was a French Soldier [Jean Pierre] fighting with Napoleon. The army adored him, worshipped him like a god'.

Interestingly, in this Life, two personalities were fighting one another, experiencing both sides of the coin [multiple Incarnations.] [15.6.15]

173.A Galleon White Sails[17] 17/18th Century

Something is stirring inside my solar plexus as I start the regression. I feel very uneasy and begin to feel upset. I take a few breaths. The discomfort increases. My vision becomes blurred as I withdraw to an Inner Place.

'There was a Death which went undetected for some time' comes through, 'and the face of a man, perhaps in his early 30s, suddenly appears. He has longish dark- blond hair, moustache and short dark-brown beard.Quite attractive. He wears clothes [cape, trousers, knee-long boots, hat] like the Three Musketeers, seems to be aboard a galleon. I see the interior of a wooden cabin under the helm of the ship. 17th century? 18th century?

I also see another man, perhaps in his 40s, with large hat, flowing mantle, large 'puffy' sleeves and breeches, long boots. He has a strong face, long black curly hair and moustache; small triangular beard. He is aboard a ship, white sails, oil-smooth sea, while half-naked men are handling ropes. He wears a long, white, pointed collar and sleeve cuffs. Spanish? French?

Pirates-Battle at Sea

Something is happening. The vessel has been blocked by another ship and a rope bridge thrown across, over which rough, violent men [pirates] brandishing swords and muskets run aboard the galleon. There is a fierce fight. Many are dead, but the pirates are thrown back, their ship has been hit and has a big hollow on the side but it manages to slip away. Their bodies are dropped overboard, while others await on the deck a burial at sea by their Captain. I now see the younger, dark-blond, man.

His head is turned and is looking at me.' [29.8.17]

Victorian England

26.Life in Victorian London

'A husband, a businessman in his early 40s, not very tall and dressed in a black suit, dark haired, came home earlier than usual. The wife, a beautiful woman in her late 30s, just managed to get dressed and her younger lover disappeared into the attic in his pants.

The wife asked her husband if he was going to visit some friends that night, but he said no, so she asked: 'Are you going to be here all night?' He looked a bit surprised and then said 'Yes'. They then spoke about a daughter, who might have died, because the wife said 'She is gone'. Before the man left for the bedroom, he saw something on the floor and picked it up: it was a man's necklace and exclaimed: 'Is this not Edward's?' The wife said yes, Edward was doing all sort of things in the house.

In the morning, the husband got up and told his wife he could not sleep all night. 'There must be mice in the attic because there was some noise' and he went up to see for himself. His wife tried to dissuade him-at last he left the house and she went up the attic calling 'Edward, Edward'. The window was open and Edward had gone on the roof to avoid being seen. When he was inside getting dressed, the woman told him she had money and things they could sell, so she could leave her husband and they could go to New Mexico, and so they did. He was a young man in his 20s. She cut her hair very short, like a man, and had it died black [it was long and blonde] and looked younger and good-looking. She sold a number of things, even clothes. There was a dark-pink coat, designer, she tried to sell. Meanwhile the husband was getting married and went to buy clothes. For some reason, she went back to London and someone who knew her, saw her and perhaps the husband was informed of that.' [24.10.98

65.Childhood Memories Now and Past

'I saw myself when I was perhaps 10 years old, on the

beach, on holiday and another girl, who was my friend, there with me. I still see her as I write, with beach hat, short beach dress, barefooted on the sand. I then saw myself as a 6-year-old, again on the beach on holiday. Went further back and saw myself as a baby. Going further back in time, I saw a beautiful baby with naked feet, short, sleeveless, white dress and little white cloche hat, smiling. Saw some young women, good-looking, long skirts, tiny waists, dark-brown hair combed up; very clearly, perhaps late 19th century and an elegant man, good looking, perhaps late 30s early 40s, pale grey bowler hat and pale grey coat. Saw other women, a maid with white apron, all very clearly'. [23.7.13]

Charlotte Bronte [1816-1855]

33.An Unexpected Appearance

'I saw Charlotte Bronte[128]. She had light-brown, soft. straight hair, parted in the middle, falling down her cheeks, taken up nicely at the back of her head. She is not a beauty, but has a very interesting face and piercing clever eyes. The expression in the portrait is very correct, the portrait is a very good likeness of her. I see her in the front, she could be beautiful in proper clothes and her face done up. She has an impression on the side of the tip of her nose like mine, but more pronounced, not unpleasant. '

99.A Glimpse-A Surprise

Suddenly, out of nowhere, Charlotte Bronte[70] appeared as she was later in life, and she is still here with me now as I write. She also recently came to me briefly.

100.Dreams and Disappointment

Did a two-hour Regression Therapy, one of the most complete so far. 'I was Charlotte Bronte. I saw her in her late

20s, as she was in her portrait. She went through her life-saw the moors and children playing, the Parsonage at Haworth, her Father, a good-looking man with white hair, tall, quite fit. Saw the house, small rooms, adolescents full of intellectual activity and wild dreams, three girls and a boy: Charlotte, Anne, Branwell, Emily.

Saw Charlotte with a pretty bonnet and in travelling clothes, really pretty, perhaps 19 years old, enjoying the prospect of travel and adventure. Saw the school she went to in Brussels, a beautiful large building on large grounds; the Church in the square and went inside, quite dark, to the Confessional, Charlotte quite upset. Then back to England, feeling shattered.

Out of the crisis came 'Villette' and trips to London, to the editor, Smiths. The book under the name of Currer Bell was very successful, money coming in and further trips to London. What a change from Haworth!

A Love which Was Not Love-Death [1855]

There was that priest who fell in love with me, I did not like him at first, but his persistence convinced me it was love. A new phase of my life was opening up, so I thought and so it did, though not how I would have expected it. That man brought me death. My delicate body could not cope with the stress of a pregnancy. I got ill with consumption and died soon afterwards.

I saw Charlotte in her bed, very ill and weak, drifting in and out of consciousness, in pain, the sadness of it all! It nearly broke my heart. After her passing I saw only Darkness. I saw Charlotte in her narrow coffin, Haworth Parsonage-dismal in the rain.

I have an overwhelming feeling of bitterness, incompleteness and sorrow. I feel upset, unsettled. I only saw Darkness, deep Darkness.' Could not get the last thought, nor whether she went into the White Light. Something tried to release itself as there was a tremendous pull from my viscera upwards to the throat charka it nearly choked me, but nothing happened. I felt it twice and thought my heart would break. I was extremely upset for days. [20.5.15]

101.Currer Bell: Fame

'Charlotte was there waiting for me and I became her. My heart missed a few beats, there was sadness. I was dressed elegantly, with a lovely bonnet tied with a ribbon under my chin. I was in London, a huge building with very high ceilings and large halls, an exhibition, full of people. What a contrast from Haworth!

Regrets-Death-A Release

'I asked Charlotte to give me her thoughts, lot of sorrow after the deaths of Branwell and Emily, the last one particularly traumatic, 'the end of all childhood's dreams.' I went to the death scene and felt very heavy, slowing down, but no thoughts, no matter how hard I tried, just Darkness.

Again, I went to the death scene and eventually I saw a mist rising from the body and it stood there for some time. I brought the Light to the body and felt a very strong pull from deep into my viscera, rising strongly towards the throat charka towards the Light. I let the Light flood the body in a shaft of White Light and on myself, and something went up into the Light and I heard a faint 'Thank you. 'All went peaceful. Charlotte is here behind me as I write, she is part of me. I feel relieved.' [21.5.15]

139.The End of All Dreams-Last Moments

My Father-in World War One uniform-appeared, and then my Mother, to guide me to a Past Life.

'I went back to Victorian England, when I saw a young woman with dark hair parted in the middle, long skirt and long-sleeved blouse, tucked in at the waist, and a small triangular scarf on her shoulders, large eyes, not beautiful, but attractive, small frame, Charlotte Bronte.

I see a young Charlotte, Emily, Anne, like that famous painting. I feel sick in my stomach. I see a dying Charlotte in her bed, weak, covered in sweat, fully conscious of what is happening, her hair loose on the pillow.' I feel agitated and sick as I experience her last moments.

'I cry, I am in pain, I am angry. I feel my grasp on life is loosening, life slipping through my fingers. I am afraid. That hateful man is by my side. Why did I marry him? I thought it was love. It was not. I deceived myself.' I feel the pain, the intensity of that moment. Anger, resentment, betrayal. Great pain in the stomach. Did you accept you were dying? I ask.

'No. Like Emily, I fought to the last. My eyes became blurred as I slipped into unconsciousness and eventually passed on. I see the young Charlotte of that painting, again her eyes full of hope and expectation, eager for love.' I feel the pain of the unfulfilled promise. I am overwhelmed by it.

'I see Charlotte as a young woman, successful, her large, clever eyes full of hidden sadness, of understanding of life.' Great pain in the solar plexus.

'All life is an illusion created by us.' [13.7.15]

Queen Victoria [1819-1901]
Princess Alice [1843-1878]

96.A Palace Reception

'Suddenly, Victoria[63] is here, wearing a tiara, a white evening dress, diamond necklace, bracelets and a blue ribbon across her chest.' She was with me a long time and would not go away, she is still here as I write, in front of me.

A Short Life [1843-1878]

'Then one of her daughters appeared, also wearing a white evening dress, her black hair pushed back and falling in curls around her ears, smiling, young and beautiful, and she too would not go away. I was one of Victoria's daughters and had a short life.[64]' [23.3.15]

98.Glimpses

Felt awful and ill in the last few days, palpitations, could not sleep last night, heavy heart. Something big was surfacing. 'At first saw Jesus in white tunic, dark hair and short beard, then Mary; and Jesus from above the Cross. I saw a young Victorian woman about 30 years old, like a big photograph, and a younger Victorian woman in very good clothes, possibly in her early 20s. Then Victoria dropped in and took over and became me. I saw her younger, about 40 years old, and later, she would not go away. I sent her through the Light and she went, until I only saw the outline of her head and then she disappeared.'

99.George V-Tsar Nicholas II

'I saw a large hall with majestic staircase at one end, full of Victorian aristocrats. I saw a man, but did not know whether he was George V[66] or Tsar Nicholas of Russia who were first cousins and were very much alike. I think it was George V in uniform, epaulettes, medals, a red silken scarf across his chest, blue eyes, moustache, beard. Then I saw them both together, Nicholas and George V.'

In Mourning [1861]

'I saw Victoria in her late 30s early 40s, then a young Prince Albert[67] and an older Prince Albert, Victoria in mourning and the children in black in a black carriage.[68] I saw myself in black, about 18/20 years old. Then Alice stepped forward to speak:

The death of our Father, Prince Albert, cast a dark shadow over the Palace, a feeling of gloom we wanted to escape from but could not, as our Mother retired from the world, immersed herself in her inconsolable sorrow and became more demanding towards us.' This memory brought about a second, incredibly powerful, stomach contraction forcing something big up to the throat chakra, a release which nearly choked me. I felt the bond between Victoria and me-we were very close, now I understand why she often comes to me. I can see her here opposite me as I write, her face close to mine. Could not get details of her daughter's death[69].

101.An Overwhelming Presence

Suddenly and unexpectedly, Victoria dropped in and I sent her away, but she is here as I write, and write I will.

118.Mystery Man

One-hour regression. 'Saw a tall man, portly [not fat], possibly in his early 30s, long, curly, auburn hair, richly dressed, long oval face, high cheekbones, large round eyes, long nose, full mouth with full lips, not good-looking, but not ugly, an aristocrat, a King. I wore silk shoes with buckles, knee-long silk stockings and silk breeches, waistcoat and coat. Could not discover who I was, whether French, British or Spanish. Saw men dressed in black, 'puffy' breeches, top with white pointed collars, large hats like those of Cromwell's men. Still do not know who he was.' Felt great, great unease crippling my stomach and great physical and mental exhaustion, so tired I had to lie down. [11.6.15]

119.Coburg-Gotha

A long regression, over one and a half hour.

'Immediately I saw this tall, imposing 18th Century man, as if in a life-sized portrait painting, in full regalia, silk shoes with buckles, silk stockings with knee-long breeches, long silk waistcoat, ermine cap with gold chain across his chest, long narrow face. He had round eyes, strong nose and mouth, high

forehead, and white hair combed back [not periwig] perhaps in his 40s, the same man who came to me yesterday. I saw him in a beautiful pale-blue uniform with ribbon straps across his chest, epaulettes, white periwig, much younger, wearing a military blue triangular hat with rolled up rims, and again, wearing a riding suit, large hat, darkish red-brown jacket with scarf across his chest, breeches and shoes of the same colour.' There were interferences. An almost unbearable pain came into the heart region, for a long time, I thought it would break me up, could not ascertain the nature of this pain, then it moved up into the upper chest and under the shoulders. It was so strong I could hardly breathe. Could not discover the cause of such colossal pain. 'I saw this man dead, lying on his back, by profile, looking serene. I felt stretched out and I was him'. Still the pain lingered, just as strong. Eventually, it moved up into the crown chakra, at the top of the head and I tried to force it out, do not know if I did, but suddenly it let go and the pain released. The name 'Coburg-Gotha'[97] came through, but no other details. 'I also saw him with a moustache.' I have not been able to identify him, although I saw him very clearly, he looked more like an Emperor than a King and had a face a bit like Ferdinand III, Holy Roman Emperor, although he was not him. [1608-1657] [12.6.15]

135.A Most Determined Woman

Suddenly, Victoria drops in and I ask her to leave as I want to continue with Susan, but she is most stubborn and will not do so. 'I see her dead in her coffin.' I try to shut her out. Difficult, she is used to have her way. I ignore her and carry on with Susan Owen. Victoria has become very persistent of late. It is no use. She will not go, and there is another visit.

Alice: Looking Back

'I now see myself as one of her daughters, young and beautiful, with dark hair combed up prettily, wearing another cream-white evening dress.'

138.A Lasting Bond

Victoria is here again, in full regalia [not in black, but white] and she interrupts me. 'Henrietta[101] appears, a lively, beautiful young woman, black hair and eyes.' I am annoyed.

Victoria is behind me and bends over me, protective and controlling. Even now she cannot let go of me. We were very close.

Happy Memories

'My hair is parted in the middle, falling in thick curls on the side of my oval face, large eyes, long cream-white evening dress. Palace saloons with large glass-doors open on extensive gardens. Albert is there, quite young. It seems all mixed up. A young Victoria and an old one in black, at the same time. Small children, boys with tiny suits and knee-long trousers.' I am going to stop.

143.Always with Me

'Queen Victoria suddenly appeared with tiara and full state regalia, then in black dress' very close to me. I felt her presence by my side behind me. [14.10.15]

144.An Interference

I then saw a photo of a lady dressed in white with a tiara, good-looking, perhaps in her early 30s, almost by profile, dark, curly hair combed up and parted in the middle.' I cry as I write this, feel very emotional.

A Stubborn Woman

Queen Victoria suddenly drops in a couple of times, in her middle years. I think she wants to speak through me, but I try to revert to the World War One Soldier who just dropped in. Victoria is here again, I tell her to come back later, after this Soldier's Life, but she is very stubborn. I manage to go back to the Soldier. I ask him what was his rank in World War One.

A Summer Evening

I try to continue, but Victoria is here again, very close to me, determined to stay, and so be it. She always has her way. 'I see one of her daughters, but do not recognize her. I am that daughter. I see a huge room, large glass doors open overlooking vast grounds with long curtains blown gently by a gentle breeze, all peace and tranquillity. '

161.An All-Pervading Presence

Suddenly, young Victoria steps in and I tell her to go away. I am happy to see her, but I am annoyed. She takes over. 'She is young, in a white evening dress, with a blue band across her chest, wearing jewels and tiara. I see her as an older woman, still wearing a tiara, dark dress, her face close to mine, looking straight ahead. and then she is opposite me, in dark clothes and white cape like a Spanish woman, but not looking at me.

She is now standing behind me, her hands on my shoulders. She is all around me. I am young, I am in a garden, wearing a nice, simple dress, my hair combed behind my head. I have dreamy eyes.

I see a young Victoria, a small and lovely face, pale- blue eyes, and then again, an old Victoria, white hair. She takes over and is me. She sits at her desk writing letters.

All Alone

Victoria sits in my chair, she hardly fits in, with her large frame and dress. I feel pain in my heart and ask her: 'How did you feel when Albert died?' She draws a long sigh and stares blindly ahead of her.

'I wanted to lie in a darkened room and die. I could not cope with the responsibility thrust upon me. The sight of the children annoyed me, and so did all the noise, my sensitivity heightened to excess by excessive grief. I locked myself into the recesses of my heart and delegated work.

Alice: My Rock

Alice was a great support. I wish her to know this and how much I valued her and loved her. I know now I laid my sorrow squarely on her shoulders and am sorry for it. I could not have coped without her. When she married and left me, I was devastated as if in mourning again. Life dealt me a second blow, but I sufficiently recovered in time. I loved my children in my own way, though I could not suffer them. Not all turned out well, the girls did better. Our expectations of Our children were mostly frustrated. I had a long life which I had hoped to spend with Albert, but it did not go that way-Victoria adds with a sigh. I never wanted to be Queen, but I was. Most of my expectations remained expectations.'

162.A Moment of Tenderness

'Victoria appears again, wearing a black dress and a white lace cape.' There is no keeping her away and she is with me most of the time of late. She stands in front of me and behind me, her hands on my shoulders. There is a very faint smile on her lips, reflected in her eyes. She is old. There is a strange softness in her, I never knew in my life with her. She has now replaced me and sits in my chair squeezing her large frame in it. We are One.

The Pain of Mourning

I see myself as Alice, young, fresh-faced and modestly dressed. I feel the weight of responsibility heavy on my shoulders.

'When dear Papa died, a dark Cloud hung over the Palace, our lives were never the same again as our Mother withdrew herself into darkened rooms and closed her doors on us all. I alone was allowed near her.' she says. A feeling of sadness pervades me. I see Victoria by profile, she is quite old. I feel heaviness in my heart.

'When dear Vicky left me, I could not bear it. It was a sad loss. Our family was breaking apart' she says. Prince Albert is here behind me, his hands on my shoulders. He is in his mid-30s, a few years before his death. I cannot feel his thoughts. He is now in front of me, a serious face, his head like a dome, staring intently into my eyes. I see a floating image of the children when they were small.

164.Always with Me

Even before I start the regression, Victoria is by my side, in her late years, in black and white lace cape. She is now wearing her tiara and jewels. I see Alice in evening dress and jewels, young and beautiful.

167. Confessions

Victoria is here, she is all around me, very close. I loved her dearly, but now realize how her love was oppressive, controlling, but still love.

'I see Victoria as a young widow, and Alice, both dressed in black with black hats. I see an older Victoria, still in mourning. Images of a young and old Victoria come and go.' This regression is really about her. Even now in this Life, she controls me. She sits in my chair in full regalia, tiara, diamonds, the lot. Have you something to say? I ask.

'I have been misunderstood all my life' she says with a low, plaintive voice 'nobody understood me, only Albert did.' I feel her genuine pain and am sorry for her. 'I saw the Palace like a prison I wanted to escape from' she adds. 'I got away whenever I could. I relied on trusted servants to shield me from unwanted attention. This created friction within my family, but I did not care. The devotion of one servant brought some normality in my life. I valued his company above all others.' Victoria is lost in her thoughts. I do not dare to ask any more questions.

JB-Happy Again

'I see beautiful countryside, a castle [Balmoral?], Victoria on a horse, JB by her side. She looks happy. Victoria is older now, looking back on her life.

I enjoyed his company - she suddenly says - looking straight at me, reading my mind. Lovers? No, we were not lovers in the way you think, we never went as far as that, but we were happy together, a 'marriage of minds' she adds. 'He was my equal in many ways, but never took advantage, it was all very proper, despite evil gossipers. The life he showed me is a life I would have wanted to live, had I not been Queen.' As Alice, I understand her. I, too, would have loved a simple, 'ordinary' life.'

An Ungrateful Son

'People criticised me for my unorthodox choice of companions. They envied them, resented them. They feared their loss of power. Their vanity! Did me no good. Even my son Bertie stood up against me, his Mother!-she adds with bitterness. They hated seeing me happy! When I was old and weak, they overpowered me. Mrs Brown? she asks suddenly. No, there never was a Mrs Brown, but I wish there had been!' [17.8.17]

176.Forever Mourning

Victoria, later in life, suddenly appears, dressed in black with black hat. 'Oh, that gloomy, gloomy black! It affected Us all at the Palace. It cast a shadow on Us Children, and on everyone else. We had to endure it for years!

Victoria and JB

Now I see Victoria on a horse, younger, and always in black, with JB[122] holding the reins of the horse, looking pleased. Bertie, my dear Brother, appears, a grown-up man. I do not know what to make of all this. Bertie's face is very close to mine. I see Alice in travelling clothes, also with a hat. I am her, now, and She write this. She is now in front of a large building and there is a large, stately, room. Alice, do you want to say something? I ask her. I feel I am not getting anywhere and want to close. Louis is in the background, and Bertie appears again, by my side. It is all very confusing.

Bertie in Paris

I see an older Bertie[106] portly, top hat and cigar, stepping out of a carriage in Paris. Victoria frowns. I feel her disappointment and her displeasure. I know where he is going, and so does She.'[106] [5.9.17]

Alice Of Hesse [Married 1 July 1862]

164.Straight from her Heart

Are you happy? I ask her. Alice becomes me, and sits quietly in my chair. Young Victoria in the background. I ask her not to interfere and stay there. Are you happy, Alice? I ask again. A cloud passes over her face. In the background I see her husband, Louis, young and good- looking.

'When I married, I was the happiest woman in the world, though I could not show it. I felt I had achieved all I wanted to achieve in life. But it was a disappointment. I wanted a soulmate, someone I could share my inner thoughts with, but it was not to be. We could not be more dissimilar in our perception of the world around us. A bitter disappointment, but I truly loved my husband and made the most of my marriage. We had lovely children and I loved them dearly. It was a good life, though not what I had hoped for. I was not happy in the limiting circles of my new home and longed to escape from it. I busied myself with public work. The War gave me plenty of opportunities for this, which were often frown upon. Even the Queen was averse to this, but I did not care. Louis was behind me, supporting me. I met remarkable people, Florence Nightingale[117] one of them. They all enriched my life, opened my horizons.' Alice suddenly pauses, lost in thoughts.

'Victoria and I grew further and further apart[117]' she adds with a sigh. 'It was painful to me, but we were so different. I could not help disagreeing with her and stood my ground. She called me 'obstinate' and I am sure she too suffered in this widening rift. In the end, we hardly spoke, or wrote, to one another. The Prince of Waleswas another such disappointment for our Mother. We could not help it. I loved Bertie and sympathized with him.' Were you very unhappy? I ask softly.

'I was not very unhappy, but was not happy either. Life had not turned out the way I expected. Sometimes it was harder to accept than others, but I coped with it. As a girl, I dreamt of falling passionately in love and l ive of love forever. But a girl's dreams are not a woman's reality. I discovered that soon enough' she adds with some bitterness in her voice. 'Louis was a good husband and I loved him, but he was not my soulmate. He loved me dearly and supported me in what I did, but he was not an intellectual and I missed this. We often visited Mother before we drew apart, as I needed to escape from the limitations of my home. Things then changed! The War[117] changed everything, even the love between me and Vicky![115] That was painful. The death of my children[118] brought another dimension to our lives. It was very difficult to take in.' I feel an overwhelming wave of sadness. Alice stops and stares vacantly in front of her, lost in her thoughts. I feel the pain.

'It is hard for a mother to see her child die' she adds after a while. 'I thought my life would end, but I survived for my other children, though not for long.' How did you feel when you knew you were dying? I whisper.

'It happened suddenly and I did not linger long enough to think about it'. Alice is overwhelmed by the intense pain of this memory, which I fully feel in my heart. I can hardly breathe, such a strong emotion.

'As I lay in my bed, Life fleeing from me, I had a vision: all of us, children, around our dear Papa and Mama. I was distraught at leaving my children, but leave them I did, as I sank into unconsciousness and died. I hovered there a long time and was distressed to see their pain.' A long silence follows which I break when I suddenly ask: 'Did you have many regrets?'

'Oh, yes!' Alice replies 'many!' But she will not say which. I feel the Darkness come over us and I know I must leave her now, but her pain is in my heart. Strangely, throughout the regression the name 'Wuttemberg' came up several times and even 'Alice of Wuttemberg' - this does not make sense to me. [14.8.17]

165.Hospital Nurse

'I see Alice as a young woman, her hair neatly combed in tresses behind her head. I see Bertie as a young man. Suddenly, I feel extremely hot.

I see Alice[117]working in a makeshift hospital, chaotic, white beds everywhere, mattresses on the floor, Alice and other nurses walking carefully among them, tending the wounded. There is noise, a lot of moaning, blood-stained bandages. My heart feels sore. The wounded lie in a large room with high ceilings and arch-like windows through which light pours in, revealing hidden corners and suffering. Suddenly, I see Alice in a different setting, in a large stately room, with a long dress, folding in the front, standing near a marble fireplace, lost in thoughts.' My stomach suddenly contracts with growing pain. It takes my breath away. I ask her to tell me what this pain is.

A Child's Death

'The Reality of War gave me a taste of what Death was like, but I was not prepared for the death of my child' she whispers. 'I cannot forget the long, sleepless nights, the Silence and Mute fears that followed its death; the overwhelming sense of loss and despair which came over us. Victoria, too, was stunned into grief. It was an impossible hard time, impossible to describe' she adds with a sigh. I do not dare to ask questions such is the intensity of her feelings. My Mother appears and I ask her help. I feel Alice's pain deep inside myself. 'Little did I know my Time also was running out, she whispers, lost in thoughts. Soon I would leave my Children and all I had fought so hard for.' I am beginning to feel tired and urge Alice to speak. Her Sorrow rises with the rising tide of her emotions. I feel sick. I urge her to release them. Why do you not let them go? I ask softly. 'Because they keep me here and, in a strange way, I do not want to let them go-she answers. But why do you want to stay here, there is nothing for you here, I say. I am mystified. Your family is all in Spirit, there is nothing for you here, or is there? What was your last thought? I ask softly.

A Painful Death

'I see Alice on her deathbed, pale and feverish, her hair loose on her pillow, sifting in and out of consciousness, struggling with her breath. It is not a peaceful passing.' Alice, what was your last thought? I ask again, but I am tired and I am going to close the session. [15.8.17]

166.Unhappiness

'Isee Alice as a young woman, her mass of black hair neatly combed back, wearing a long-sleeved dress and large flowing gown.' I am her and there is heaviness in my solar plexus. Feel the pain and let go. What is wrong, Alice? I ask softly.

Alice/Catherine: Parallel Lives

Quite unexpectedly, I see both Alice, and my former Incarnation, Catherine Parr, with the tail of my eye. They all had similar temperaments, ambitions. They both were disappointed, frustrated, in their lives. Catherine dropped in yesterday, but I sent her away. I feel the pain and frustration of their unfulfilled ambitions, of their quest for love. Catherine and Alice had very short lives, they both died aged 36. I feel their disappointment.

Regrets

'If I had lived in your time' Alice tells me- 'I would not have married, much as I loved my husband and children. I would have pursued a career, become a doctor, travelled the world, broken down barriers and taken up women's causes. Too big an ambition? -she asks with a smile. Women were so repressed and frustrated in their hopes, and most lived in their husbands' shadow, though I did not.

Mother was against me [Victoria is listening in the background], she did not understand me and was appalled at my plain speaking and directness of certain aspects of life she found difficult to discuss so openly, which I did not. We were so different. I upset her many times later in life and as I grew stronger in my convictions, I resented more and more her control on my life and distanced myself from her. It was not easy at first, but as her dislike of my actions and the things I did and said grew with her, she loosened her grip on me and let me go.

I resented her, I resented her, I resented her!' she says, in a temper. I am surprised. 'She controlled our lives, she despised us, she cast a shadow on our childhood, but there was love. Our parents loved us, but their love was very strict, full of their expectations for us. I loved my parents very much, especially my Father. I was modest and subordinate. Only later in life I became conscious of the strain we were all under. The boys suffered most. [Bertie is here with me as I write this and watches every word] The rift with Bertie was insuperable, though, at the very end, our Mother showed a rare quality, a Mother's love.'

Alice pauses, lost in her thoughts. 'Bertie and I were very close. I stood by him whenever I could. I felt he was badly treated by both Our parents. I tried to be a good mother to my children and hope they remembered me with love.' What a long speech! Alice is silent now, but I wonder whether she wants to say more. I do not know what to ask her. 'Yes, I hope my children remembered me better than I remembered my Mother'-there is some resentment in her voice which surprises me, 'but I loved her and my early death [the first of her long-lived children] truly affected her. She felt pure love for me breaking out of her all too powerful need to control. I see it now.' she concludes. [16.8.17]

174. A Wedding like a Funeral[120]

Even before I start the regression, Alice is here with me, beautiful in white wedding dress, no veil, jewels and tiara. She looks down, hands folded on her gown. There is pain in my solar plexus and the heart chakra. 'Our wedding was like a funeral, joyless, Our Father having died a year ago. We wanted to postpone it, but Our Mother insisted that it should take place, although with little ceremony. It was brief. Our Mother stood in a corner of the room, dressed in black. It was painful to her, another loss she felt bitterly. I could not console her. We left with a mixture of regret and relief.' Alice concludes, with a long pause.

A Life of Disappointment

'When we reached Our destination, I was dismayed by what I saw, so different from my home, so backward and dismal. I would escape from it as much as I could. Mama needed me still and insisted that I visit her often. In the first years of my marriage, I spent more time with her than in my new home, and was glad of it. I felt I did not fit in with the small talk and mentality of the people who surrounded me.' Alice is a natural talker and her thoughts flow freely through my pen. 'It did not take long for me to understand the reality of my situation and become disenchanted, but I loved Louis and made the most of it. I busied myself with unpopular activities, with work deemed unsuitable for a Princess and future Duchess, but I was a rebel by nature, and persevered with Louis' support. He was very good and eager to please me, though he did not understand me.

As my rift with my Mother deepened, I got more involved in public work at home and I even met an intellectual Soulmate[121], someone I could discuss things I could not with my husband. This gave me fresh energy to invest in my work, but it all came to an end. More changes were on the way.

The death of Louis' Father threw more responsibilities on Our shoulders. Little did I know' she adds with a sigh 'that my time, too, was running out.' I feel her distress and ask softly: What is it that pains you so much, why not let it go?

'I wish my life had been different, but I do not regret having children, they were a joy to me. I wish I had been a man, more in command of my life. Why do I linger? What is this pain I steel feel?' she asks looking at me. 'I do not know, perhaps the incompleteness of that Life, unfulfilled, of what it could have been and was not.' Alice whispers, her voice dying down. [30.8.17]

179.Trying to Connect

I have been feeling quite anxious in the last few days and I know there is a Past Life surfacing. So, as I sit quietly, I sink deeper and deeper into the Sands of Time. I feel the tension around that Life, which I still do not know. I feel the tension right up my chest, under the collar bone, something deeply seated and reluctant to come up. I have been doing this for over an hour, I am tired and I am going to stop. [22.9.17]

183.Victoria

Now I see Victoria. It is all mixed up, like crossing telephone lines. I feel great pain in my heart chakra. I continue the regression and her daughter appears.

With an open Heart

'The death of Our Father traumatized me. I loved him very much. His death was like a dark cloud which hung on Us all. It brought me even closer to my Mother and I took it upon myself to help her through her sorrow. I became indispensable to her. I still feel Our pain. The Palace became a place of Sorrow as Our Mother withdrew within herself and shunned Us all, except myself. I was her secretary, friend and confidante, despite my young age. I felt I was old. I had none of the gaiety of girls of my age. I rarely smiled, so conscious of my duties and commitments. I comforted my Mother and helped her through her depression and moments of despair. I felt sorry for her. I loved her very much, but she suffocated me with her Grief, with her Self-Pity, with her demands on my time. I felt I became an appendage to her will, a helpless receptacle into which she poured her thoughts, frustration and despair. My caring nature made me the perfect recipient of all this. My youth, and the demands of my youth, disappeared. I lived in her shadow. Only now, in this new Life, I realize the weight of her demands on me. I do not regret being her companion and her solace, but the weight of it all shatters me now. I still feel her influence, as she is never far from me, even in this new Life. I love her still and she knows it.

When I got married, she felt betrayed, although she was in favour of it. She reached out to me even after that. I felt for her and her loneliness, for loneliness it was and remained so for many years. My Life then was not very happy[123], but not entirely unhappy either. It was a disappointment. I loved my Children very deeply and when one died, it took a part of me away with it. Death was a relief for me, in some way, though I was upset at leaving my Children behind.

Did I learn something from that Life? I do not know. One thing I know. My Child's death left a very deep trauma in my Soul and I still feel the pain after so many years. Victoria still has demands on my time and is often with me [she is here now behind me with crinoline and jewels] as I write. I still love her [and miss her].

Life did not turn out as I expected, but then it never does, and I did not expect anything at the time. I was happy with my Family, dearly loved my Father, and still do, and miss him through the Ages. Will I ever get over this?' I feel there is much more behind this but stop. [11.1.18]

Chapter 16

Nicholas II of Russia [1868-1918]

53.A Doomed Man

I TRIED FOR over one hour to do a regression and nearly gave up, despite some bad pain in my solar plexus, when something incredible happened.

'I saw a rather attractive, medium height [perhaps 1.70 m] moustachioed man of around 35 years, with blue eyes and blondish hair, in dark-blue uniform with epaulettes and medals and something like a golden 'rope' across his chest, from one shoulder to the other. I was baffled as to who he was. Eventually I recognized him and could not believe it! It was Tsar Nicholas of Russia[30] murdered with his whole family by the Soviets in 1910. [25.6.13]

A Cruel Death [1917]

'I saw the Zarina,[31] the children,[32] the eldest daughter and Anastasia, and the young boy, all in that basement, the steps going down, and that terrible bloody assassin coldly shooting them and the blood flowing! I saw the blood-covered corpses taken out of the building and dropped into a vehicle, the empty basement with blood- stained floor. What a terrible sight!'

This felt more like Rescue Work. It went on for some time and I was very, very deeply moved and distressed by the memory of their death. I closed with a few prayers.

127.A Short Visit

Out of the blue, Tsar Nicholas appeared, very close and very clear. I was so surprised. I told him I was in a Past Life and closed the session. [22.6.15]

Chapter 17

World War One[124] [1914-18]

47.On the Attack

'BRITISH SOLDIERS FROM World War One. Round hats, heavy shoes, short trousers and legs in 'bandages' up to the knee, going on foot on the attack, holding rifles. Bombs raining down on all sides, lead-coloured sky. Sudden blasts of explosions and lights.

81.A Soldier Somme Battlefield

I decided to lie down and do an energy-scan to see if I have 'intrusive energy' [spirit attachments]. I started from the feet, slowly going up, when I reached the left shoulder things began to happen.

'A man appeared, in his 30s/early 40s, wearing a dark [bluish] suit, although I only saw his shoulders. Dark hair cut short and a longish face, not unpleasant. We were both surprised, as we stared at one another for some time. I could only discover that he was a Soldier, was shot in the head and died on the battlefield. I saw him, or thought it was him, as a Soldier in uniform, legs like bandages Somme Battlefield[53], saw the frontline.

A Mixed Bag-Shot in the Head:

'I saw Tutankhamun and Ankhesenamun. Saw him as a boy, sweet and beautiful, then a Polish Officer in uniform, very attractive and smart, and a German Soldier, at least I thought he was German, with helmet, and think it was World War Two. He too was shot in the head and his brain was splattered all over the battlefield'.

I felt the presence of these Soldiers [and the pressure!] all over my body, but especially over the chest, in the heart area, very heavy. I wanted to know more but it was difficult. Did they have regrets or fears?

Earthbound

'Yes, they were scared all the time. The World War One Soldier was from Dublin. I was that Soldier. I saw him younger, in civilian clothes, wearing a beret.'

I told them several times that they were dead-I saw skeletons- that that life was over and they almost certainly had incarnated into other lives. I told them they did not have a physical body, but had attached themselves to me and asked them to be at peace and release themselves from the earth plane. I said a few prayers and asked the Higher Spirits and my own Family and Guides to help them in this, but they did not want to leave. Very, very, difficult. It went on for over two hours and the pressure on my heart charka was overwhelming. I went into their pain and trauma and brought it up to be burnt and transformed by the White Light. I brought the Light into the dark well of their despair and my heart area swelled up as if to burst open. I asked again what did they want me to do to release them, but to no avail. I told them that their families and friends were also in Spirit and waiting for them to join them. I visualized the Light going through my head and slowly all over my body, and the Virgin Mary wearing a crown, appeared at the top of my headto direct the White Light all over my body. I also saw a Cardinal dressed in dark purple, but did not recognize him. I visualized these Soldiers going up towards the Light, but do not know if they did since I did not see them doing that and I finally ended the session. [22.8.13]

140.An Officer

'My body is changing into that of a World War One

Officer. I feel the solidity of that body and faintly see a face of a man, perhaps late 20s or early 30s, good features, with a moustache. Now I am him, but have no idea of who I am. I am sitting in my chair in full uniform and hat, I feel the jacket with pockets on my chest, it is very real. Am I wearing long black leather boots? I am confused. I see this man's face clearly, wearing a round hat with some stripes, or something, in the front.' Very confusing. I have to stop. [14.7.15]

144.Through a Bookshop to a Past Life

Yesterday I entered a bookshop and was drawn to some History books on World War One and World War Two and skipped through the pages of the former, full of photographs of Soldiers and places. It filled me with great sadness. That night I slept very little, felt very depressed, so first thing in the morning I did a regression.

'Immediately I saw a young Soldier [World War One], tall, blond, long hair at the top but cut short and sculpted from top ears down the nape of the head, parted on one side, good-looking. He looks about 24 years old. I am that Soldier.' I suddenly cry. 'Images of desolation, of a battlefield, bodies strewn all over, phantom-like trees burnt down looking like stunted teeth, lead-coloured sky, profound devastation and horror.

'The World War One Soldier was also an Irish pilot in North Africa and First Lieutenant of HMS Sikh in World War Two. I see him very clearly and he is smiling. I was these men. Three different Lives, three very short Lives. What a waste!'

I see the face of the young WWI Soldier, but cannot reconnect and end the regression. [24.11.15]

Chapter 18

Wilfred Owen [1893-1918]

108.Crying Over the Past

THIS WAS A long regression, the first of many, it lasted one and a half hour. I felt very, very tense, with a very heavy heart, so much so that I feared it would break under the strain. I saw a young Soldier whom I did not know. Later looked up World War One on the net and saw a portrait of Wilfred Owen[79] whom I recognized immediately. I was overcome with extreme emotion. He was only 25 years old when he died. 'Wilfred Owen appeared in uniform, straight hair parted on the side, thin moustache and pale-blue eyes, good- looking. I saw trenches, men fighting, the sudden light of explosions. Wilfred started to cry. 'A big man crying' flashed through the mind. I was in uniform sitting on my chair, intense heaviness in my heart. I asked: 'How did you die, what was the last thought?'

'There was no time to think, blown up, the end' he replied.[80] I did not discover whether the Soul went to the Light or whether parts of it were still there where he died. I felt the trauma of his death, had a few releases, something very strong rising from deep within to the throat chakra, the crown chakra, and out into the Universe. Then, suddenly, a cry from the heart:

'The Futility of War!'

Wilfred was still sitting in my chair, the pain eased a little, but it was still there. He spoke with great bitterness, the horrors of the war forever imprinted in his soul, unable to forget and be at peace. 'We believed in the war, never having experienced it, we misled ourselves and we were misled. A whole generation. What a waste!' [30.5.15]

109.Early Life

As soon as I started, Wilfred Owen appeared and he became me and he is now writing this account of the regression, just over one-hour long.

'I saw Wilfred as a 7-year-old boy, wearing a 'sailor's-style suit, knee-long trousers, and a wide square blue top with white lines as they used in Victorian times, similar to modern-day Royal Marines uniforms. Then I saw an old Victorian lady dressed in black [grandmother] and a young girl looking a bit like the actress Cheryl Lunghi when she was young. Saw her also as a young woman, beautiful and smiling, with a light emanating from her – perhaps his sister Mary.

I saw the Battlefield, Soldiers fighting, trenches. Lord Kitchener with his big moustache and his finger pointing at you. Saw him very close and very clearly'.

Deception

Suddenly, I felt a wave of bitterness coming over me.

'How we were deceived! But we also deceived ourselves.' Felt something very oppressive grabbing and twisting my stomach. It moved up towards the crown chakra followed by a release from the head, but the pain and the anguish were still there, deeply ingrained in his Soul.

'Even without deception we would have fought in the end, so perhaps it made no difference whether we were deceived or not.

'The Futility of War!'

The human suffering; the trauma of war, naively not what we expected when we joined the ranks. WHAT did we expect?

I saw the riverbank where I was shot and died and my stomach twisted and heaviness fell over me. That a place of such beauty could see so much brutality and blood!'

The Last Thought

Wilfred was silent, overcome with emotion. I tried to get the last thought before he was shot, but could not. Eventually, with a very heavy heart, a cry: 'Mother!'

I asked Wilfred if that was his last thought and he said 'Yes'. I insisted, was it really your last thought or am I making it up? Raise my left hand if it was, I will not lift it for you. You have to do it yourself.

For a while nothing happened.

'Difficult' came through. I did not move. Eventually, my fingers very slowly moved a little, then my left hand moved a bit with difficulty, then it raised a centimetre or two with great effort, and then it went right up with force, my hand fully open, truly amazing! There was great pain in my solar plexus, I was lost in it, the memory of it all. I felt the Soul had not gone into the Light, but parts of it were still behind where I died.

A Bitter Waste

'The Futility of Human Life! I only lived half of it, or less. I never experienced the rest. My Life, an unfulfilled promise, and so were the Lives of my Friends.'

There was such overwhelming bitterness and despair in Wilfred's voice that I could not deal with it. I wish I could have given his life back. I was getting tired, so I said: 'Owen, I am getting tired with all these emotions. Come back tomorrow and share your thoughts with me. I love you, Wilfred, you can trust me, because you are me and I am you.' He started crying and could not stop. I want to release his Soul. [30.5.15]

110.A Happy Child

I decided to work on Wilfred on a daily basis, because I felt he desperately needed help. This regression lasted one-hour and even before I started, he was there waiting for me and I became him. He is writing this.

'I saw Wilfred as a toddler, blond, full round face like a

cherub, little hands and naked little feet, sitting in a baby's chair, wearing a little cap, beautiful. Saw him older, perhaps 4 or 6 years old, dressed in blue, knee-long trousers and top, looking up with sunshine in his eyes.

A Death Scene

Saw the riverbanks where he was shot, the battlefield, soldiers fighting'. I asked Wilfred to tell me if the Soul went into the Light, could not get an answer.

'Everything went pitch dark- Death.' Something stirred up from deep inside me. 'Saw the Grim Reaper riding the battlefield against a dark livid sky, bodies piled up on one another, scattered everywhere. The horror of it all!'

I felt sick in my stomach. Still did not see the Soul rising, leaving the body. It is still there. [1.6.15]

111.A Brush with Death

'There was great, overwhelming sadness. I saw the Canal[80]where I was shot. I was wounded in my stomach and lying on a battlefield with a painful wound which weakened me and made me unable to move.

I saw the Fallen all around myself, many dead. I wept, such shock and horror was on me, almost tangible, and also over the battlefield. I gradually crawled away until I was out of the shock-horror wave and then fell asleep.'

Craiglockhart-Born Again

'I next awoke in a military hospital[81] with nuns with large headdresses[82] tending me.' I used to see them in meditation and did not know why. Now I do.

'I felt as if I had died and been granted one more chance, resolved I would try and make a real difference to the world from then on.' And that is exactly what he did. [2.6.15]

112.The Poet Within

'I was recovering in that hospital. I felt my strength did not come back, but resolved to teach about the Futility of War. I saw so many die. I wrote poetry and stories and started to teach the children a few hours a week. Writing was my main expression and my topic was War.'

122.The Canal

The day before I did this one-hour regression, I felt very agitated, very heavy in the chest with pain in the stomach, very sad and depressed. Even before I started, I cried not knowing why.

'I wore heavy-duty shoes with laces, 'bandaged' legs, knee-long trousers, and jacket with pockets, belt. For some time, I could not see my face, so I did not know who I was, then slowly, I saw Wilfred, saw the Canal and the trees where he was shot, saw the water, all very clearly. Wilfred was overcome with emotion, had a good cry.

A Death Experience

At a certain point, I stiffened up and then relaxed, all tension gone, body getting heavier and numb, darkness [Death].' I did not see the Soul leaving the body and going up towards the Light. [17.6.15]

123.Earthbound

Did one-hour regression in which extreme pain blanketed out all thoughts. The sadness was overpowering and impossible to describe, it made me sick for a few hours after the regression and the feeling lasted for days. Wilfred slowly emerged from darkness and looked at me. I went back into that Life. I felt his pain. I was sitting in my chair in full World War One uniform.

'Saw the Canal and the poplars, surreal.' Keep seeing the Canal because the Soul is still there. [18.6.15]

124.Unable to Let Go

Another one-hour regression. I went back into that Life as

Wilfred and was sitting in my chair in my uniform.

'Saw the Sambre again, the poplars and the Canal. It looked so peaceful. I felt great anger and the grip of despair hitting my stomach, an almost unbearable wave of anxiety filling my chest. I felt the pain and sorrow of the Soldiers who died with me whose Souls are still there, in fragments, like mine, unable to overcome the shock and trauma of their deaths.' I brought some White Light on the Sambre to clear the area and start the process of releasing them. [19.6.15]

125.The Pain of Disillusionment

One-hour regression. Immediately Wilfred came in. I went back to that Life and was sitting in my chair in my World War One uniform. I saw Wilfred as a boy. There is vast pain, bitterness, and sorrow, which is holding parts of his Soul behind. I tried to find out what it was, so we could release it. Was it disappointment, anger, regret? Could not wade through the mayhem of his emotions. I questioned him several times to no effect. Then, suddenly there was a cry:

'Everything I believed in, collapsed at the Front. A great price to pay!' I felt engulfed in tremendous deep pain twisting my stomach and slowly filling my chest right up to the collarbone, breathing was difficult. Impossible to describe the utter totality of this pain. It left me exhausted, but gradually it decreased in intensity.

'The Futility of War!'

Wilfred sat quietly in my chair, enjoying some peace and the Light flashing on him. It will take quite an effort to release those parts of his Soul which linger on.

A Burning Question

'Gay? Ridiculous!'[100]

I felt very sore in my chest and in my stomach, like an open wound. Wilfred is uneasy and restless. He is very angry. Why?

'Some people claim with absolute certainty that I was gay.

They read and misread my poetry and reach the wrong conclusions. Why, did I know them, did they know me? They mistake intellectual affinity with sexual affinity. I naturally looked up to other poets I admired, people of my age with whom I identified and felt we had a lot in common. I did not have much time for women, though I admired a few. My Life was too short' he concludes with bitterness. I too am very upset. [20.6.15]

126.A Respite

One-hour long regression. Slowly, Wilfred appeared and we merged. I felt calmer than I have been in the last few days and did not want to press him too much with questions. The pain has diminished, and much has been released. 'I felt so tired that I had to lay to lie down on my bed in my uniform and shoes. I felt the impact of my Officer's hat on my pillow.' [21.6.15]

127.Regrets

A regression over one-hour long. Wilfred appeared and we became one. I asked him if he had any regrets and immediately realized what a silly question it was.

'Regrets? Yes, I have many. I was not ready to die. We were totally unprepared for what we saw at the Front, the carnage, the brutality of War, there is no glory in it!'

I went into his pain like entering the dark mouth of a big black monster. The more you advance, the stronger it becomes. I double up in pain. I suddenly ask: What happened immediately after Death?

'My Soul was catapulted out of my body. I looked around and only saw devastation and death, the debris of war. Wilfred is kneeling over the bodies of his Soldiers, his Officer's hat in his left hand.' I feel the strain of all this, where is the Light? Oppressive pain in the stomach.

A Release?

'Suddenly, I see a huge vortex of Light in the sky and Wilfred going into it, full uniform, no hat, like Superman, head first, arms close to the body. The Light encompasses everything in round circles. 'Thank you' comes through. I see a multitude of Souls, Soldiers in uniform, rising from the bodies on the Sambre, going up towards the Light', but the pain lingers and I feel the full impact ofit.

128.Looking Back

Another hour-long regression. Even before I started, I felt anxiety in my stomach, and did not know why.

'I first saw a young boy, perhaps 15-years-old, for some time. Gradually, the lower parts of the body of a World War One Soldier sitting in my chair began to emerge, but could not see who it was, the upper body still deeply in shadow. Eventually, it was Wilfred. Again, I saw the Sambre, its banks and the poplars.' I told him to walk with me through the Valley of Death, and tell me what holds him back there, and he became me.

'A good-looking woman appeared, possibly in her 30s, hair combed back, then a family group and the focus fell on a young boy to the left of the group, possibly seven or eight years old, Wilfred.' The pain intensified, I felt sick. Several times I saw my Grandfather and my Mother, who is always with me, and asked their help to get him through this, so I could release him. It took time and effort. 'Saw the Sambre again, the grass on its banks squashed and messy, a battle going on, bodies here and there and everywhere, a mess.'

Falling into Death

I wanted to go through Death, but could not do it, as there was too much trauma involved in it. After some time, I saw a Dark Shadow under a Black Mantle and inside it a Skull [Death]. Everything went pitch black and I fell deeper and deeper into Blackness, literally 'falling' down, further and further down into it, down into a bottomless well. It was all black, not uncomfortable, no feelings, no thoughts., it seemed to go on forever. Then, suddenly, the Darkness broke into Light, glorious Light, and I saw a shaft of intense White Light coming down from the Universe, from Heaven, shining on Wilfred's head and bathing his uniformed body in it. The Shadow was still behind him, but the Light engulfed him. I told Wilfred to let go, there was nothing to hold him back there, his Family was in Spirit and so was he. [24.6.15]

129.A Bitter Man

I got up early, had coffee and started a regression as I felt deep stomach pain and anxiety. I went back to Life as Wilfred Owen and felt the weight of great oppression all over my chest.

'I saw the Sambre again and the poplars and knew parts of my scattered Soul were still there.' The pain was so strong, it was unbearable. I went through the process of cleansing, but it only partially worked. I had to release the trauma and the thoughts and the dark mass of guilt associated with them. I then started another technique of release, went into the deep well of his pain and anxiety and brought it up with difficulty. I repeated this process many times until the pain gradually diminished, each time feeling more exhausted and gutted as if my entrails were taken out. This trauma was brought up to fever pitch intensity and slowly released as I 'vomited' the thoughts associated with the trauma:

'The loss of Innocence. When I first killed another Soldier, I lost my Innocence. Regrets. Guilt at killing another Being, destroying His Hopes and Dreams.' Again, I 'vomited' a dark mass of guilt and the thoughts associated with it.

'Guilt at the loss of Innocence. Feelings of Betrayal. Loss of all my cherished Beliefs. This War destroyed all I held sacred, except the love for my Mother!'

There was great bitterness, the pain still trapped in the upper chest. Bitterness and trauma can often 'fragment' the Soul and keep parts of it behind on the Earth Plane. Releasing trauma can be very traumatic in itself. [25.6.15]

130.A Mother's Love

I felt agitated even before I began. There are fragmented parts of Wilfred's Soul which stubbornly remain on the Sambre and refuse to let go.

'This senseless War! '

I saw Wilfred as an 18/19-year-old, and as a baby in his Mother's arms.

'My Mother and the love that binds me to Her!'

Images of a teenage Wilfred in France, timid and introvert, searching for an identity, for a profession, unfit for anything, young, idealistic and vulnerable, ill-suited to the reality of Life and War.

'My Mother, my Anchor, and my Strength. Always.'

Felt great pain in the solar plexus, a great weight pulling me down. I asked Wilfred to take me back to the War and reveal his innermost thoughts. I am beginning to feel exhausted. Susan Owen appeared and I asked her to help her Son release those parts of his Soul stuck behind. I asked Tom Owen to release his Son from the misery that ties him to this Earth Plane.

'I am sitting on the Banks of the Sambre and watch the water flow.' Hypnotic. The water flows quite fast now, a strong current. I want to stop, I am drained, but Wilfred lingers on. Intense pain in the stomach. Wilfred is in uniform and round hat sitting in my chair, watching the water flow, lost in thoughts. 'I lost my Father' The image of Christ the Redeemer suddenly appeared in a halo of White Light and took Wilfred away with Him into that Light. But Wilfred is in my chair, still earthbound. Ihave to stop. [26.6.15]

131.The Light Tunnel

As usual, Wilfred appeared in uniform and hat. I urged him to walk with me through his Death, so I can release those parts of his Soul that still remain behind. My Grandfather appeared to encourage and support me in this, and so did my Mother. Again, I felt the pain, though not as tremendous as before, but still there. Sorrow and Shock are still there. I asked Wilfred to put his hand in mine and walk with me. My open hand curled up with his and I felt a wave of emotion.

'The Sambre, the trees, the sky turned red, the colour of poppies, and blood, flowing; the fighting intensified, men were hit and dying. Overcome by the intensity of the feelings, adrenalin running high. Disaster looming, post untenable.' My hand is tightly held Wilfred's, feeling reaching fever pitch. 'Was it worth it?' I ask. 'No' he replies. I feel heaviness in my stomach spreading all over the chest and a heat-wave, turning red. Wilfred's hand still in mine. Suddenly, there is a Tunnel, like a Vortex, full of Light and a greater and more intense White Light at its end. Will he go? His hand is still in mine. Wilfred is struggling, sitting in my chair, conflicting feelings, still clasping my hand tight. Will he go?

'Your Mother is the only one who can make your Soul whole' I thought. Heaviness deeply rooted, difficult to let go. I feel tired, but Wilfred is holding on to me. 'I wish your Mother would come and help!' I think. I feel sickin the stomach. I cannot close the session. Wilfred is still holding my hand tight. I said a few prayers with him and gradually my left hand unlocked; and a few prayers for Those Who fell with him. 'Holy Father, Hallowed be Thy Name…' I feel depressed. This means Wilfred is not totally released, my left hand still blocked. 'What is holding you back?' I ask. My hand suddenly opens up, like a flower. [27.6.15]

132.Visions of Death

Great soreness in the stomach. Wilfred Owen appeared and again I asked him to walk with me through his death. He sits in my chair, his thoughts on the Sambre. There is still a lot of pain which ties him there.

'I saw the Apocalyptic Vision of the Canal, the Black sky, and Darkness falling over dead Soldiers. It was so overwhelming that I could not go any further.' [29.6.15]

133.The End of Youthful Dreams

I have not been able to regress for a few days, but even before I started, Wilfred was here, I felt his presence. After some initial difficulty, Wilfred took shape and I disappeared. He is writing this account of the regression, as usual, in uniform. Pain in the stomach. Feeling of sickness. Refusing to let go.

'I see the clear gaze of your blue eyes and the faintest glimmer of a smile on your sealed lips, holding the pain of the Reality of War imprinted on your Soul. The end of all youthful dreams. One suddenly has grown old and weary of Life.' I feel your pain, Wilfred. You are me. I feel an intense, agonising, pain twisting my heart, like a snake, and I had to stop. [3.7.15]

134.The Lion Cubs

I went back to life as Wilfred. Again, he sat on my chair in uniform and hat.

'Suddenly, the head of a lion appeared, was there for a long time. Saw the body of that lion by profile, big powerful claws. The lion became Wilfred-his head, that is, he had a lion's head and the body of a man. I felt the face of the lion on mine. I saw a cardinal, a pope, officiating Mass, also, the face of a young woman, late teens, perhaps his sister? I saw the Forestry and Soldiers crouching in the cellar, Wilfred amongst them.

The lion has reappeared, a young animal in the prime of his youth. I am sitting in a field, legs stretched out. Suddenly, I am carried through a short Tunnel filled with a tremendous White Light. I go through the Light and disappear, though I can see the faint outlines of my body.

'The lion's cubs were Wilfred's Soldiers and he felt responsible for them, beyond all calls of Duty, a very personal Bond uniting them in Life and in Death.

I see a Dark Shadow, light falls on the Sambre as night approaches, engulfing the trees, the water, and the field. I can discern only their silhouettes and a false sense of Peace.' Strong pain clutching my stomach, I feel it in all its intensity. Feel the pain and let it go.

'I looked after my Soldiers like a Mother tending her Children. I knew they were going to die-we all were! What I have seen has been imprinted on my Soul.

How can I EVER forget?'

I feel the complex feelings and emotions that still hold parts of his Soul to ransom. [5.7.15]

135.Susan Owen: The Pain of it All

Even before I started the regression, Wilfred appeared and became me.

'I see a beautiful Victorian woman in her late 40s- early 50s, elegant and slim, hair done up, looking anxious and worried [your Mother?]' I feel pain in my stomach. I become her and feel the impact of her feelings and emotions.

'She sits in my chair, wearing a long skirt and cream-white blouse, with collar and long sleeves. I feel her great pain. I see Susan Owen as an older woman, bearing her great Sorrow quietly, with great dignity. Then an older woman wearing a shawl, hair done up in tresses, around the oval of her face.' She sits in my chair, writing this. The pain and the sorrow are still there.

Nearing the End

Victoria drops in, unexpectedly. I stop the regression briefly to cut her off and Susan Owen reappears. 'I see her in bed her breathing more laboured.' Victoria re- appears, dressed in black. I cannot continue. I will stop and come back tomorrow. [6.7.15]

Death's Shadow

'I feel my life is getting closer to the end and I will be reunited with my son Wilfred' she says. Tears run down my face, the intensity of feeling overpowering. 'It has been a long journey.' I feel the pain in my stomach. My Mother, my Grandfather are with me and I ask their help to release Susan's and Wilfred's Souls from their earthly ties. 'Susan becomes weaker and tired, barely able to write. I feel weak and hot, am in a sweat. I sink deeper and deeper inside myself, withdrawing from the world.'

136.Overwhelmed

I went back to that Life and tried hard to do a regression for over one hour, but I could still feel so much pain around Wilfred, and great heaviness around the heart area that made me very tired and had to stop. [7.7.15]

138.A Distant Past

'A muddy battlefield. Horses, men fighting against a livid sky. Silhouettes. Muddy roads, the trees and the Canal'. Solar plexus and heart charkas very sore, but at least the great pain has gone. Wilfred appears, young in appearance, but old at heart. I merge with him and we are One. 'I see bodies strewn all over the field, covered with blood. What a sight! Images of happier times: a garden, foliage, a lovely house, a beautiful woman, blouse and long gown, hair combed up, children around her, husband, a family group, happy. Father with Panama hat, moustache, striped trousers. Happy days.' [10.7.15]

144.The Somme-A Glimpse

'A cavalry Officer in the Somme. I see a long row of trees in the distance, weapons and Soldiers advancing through a field, deep in mud. What a mess!'

145.A Broken Man

Wilfred unexpectedly appeared, still troubled, still bound to earth by strong emotional attachments, his own and those of his Soldiers, unable to let go and move on. His Life one of the most complex and painful I have investigated so far.

'Immediately I saw the Sambre, the long column of tall trees, the riverbanks and the water against a leaden sky.' I have a heavy heart and start crying.

'All those Lives lost, the Futility of War.' I am filled with sadness. 'I saw many Soldiers die, Friends, we were a Family, all dead'. I am sitting in my chair in uniform and officer's hat. I have a thin moustache.

'How old I have grown! I hardly recognize the youth I was, the brief Summer of happiness in Paris, all gone! War makes one old. It all seems pointless, this War. I see the tragedy of it all. These young Lives destroyed. How long will I live, another day?

My Soldiers fall around me, nothing is Sacrosanct, meaningless Faith. I stand here on the banks of Eternity and see the Waters of Time pass me by. I cannot move forward and cannot go back. A tremendous sadness weighs me down.

How used I have grown to the stench of Death, of corpses, of blood flowing, gushing from wounds, soaking the ground! I even kill with an empty heart! How different Life appears on the Battlefield!

I lost my Faith and this is tragic. What would my dear Mother think? The thought of her fills my heart, how I loved her! In those dark moments on the Battlefield, she kept my sanity, a Beacon of Light in the Nothingness of that Life.' I am overwhelmed with emotion. [9.12.15]

146.A Fragment

'I saw a young World War One Soldier near a big cannon cut against a leaden sky, slim, blond hair parted on the left side, slightly wavy, good looking, with a thin, blond moustache [Wilfred Owen?]. He is an Officer, wears a round hat, has thin, long stripes on his chest, on the left of his uniform, just above his pocket.

151.Remembering-A Tombstone in Ors

I felt a heavy pain in my upper chest. After two months, Wilfred Owen came through again, still unable to let go.

'I saw a shattered battlefield, burnt out trees, devastation all over, Wilfred traumatised and distressed. I am Wilfred Owen and his trauma lives on. I am sitting in my chair in my World War One uniform staring into nothingness in front of me. I feel tremendous pain and sorrow in my upper chest. All my Soldiers, my Brothers, are dead.

A Victorian woman, possibly in her late 30s, her hair softly taken up on the nape of her head, suddenly appears, [his Mother?] Wilfred's tombstone in Ors has a few lines from his poem 'The End: Shall Life renew/ These bodies Of a truth/ All death will he annul" [9.2.16]

157. Like A Lamb to Slaughter

It has been some time since I did a regression as I have been otherwise occupied, but I have slept so little and badly that I have decided to reduce the anxiety levels.

'Slowly, my body changed. I was wearing a World War One uniform, a round hat, jacket with pockets, belt, the lot. I saw Wilfred Owen's sweet face opposite mine and smiled. What a joy to see him again!' He is sitting in my chair, now.

'I see the Canal, a livid sky, desolation, destruction.' I have a heavy pain in my heart, my chest is heavy, I can hardly breathe.

'Like a Lamb to the Slaughter, with all my Soldiers!'

I tremble inside, the emotion is extremely powerful.

'I see Ors Cemetery.' I cry. [16.1.17]

158.A Band of Brothers

I have just come back from Ors. I am surrounded by your Soldiers, but I tell Them I only want You on this occasion.

'I see trenches, stunted trees, mud. I see the Cellar and You, surrounded by your Soldiers, Your Friends, Your Band of Brothers.'

The emotion is very strong. I cry. You are sitting in my chair, in uniform and hat. I am no longer there. You cry. I hear my voice saying, from somewhere, 'Wilfred, I am so sorry!'

'I see the Canal stretching in front of me. How beautiful and serene! How it is all changed! I see that tiny corner of

Britishness in that small country Cemetery, so peaceful, so simple and neat, not austere and sombre, so unlike any other I have seen before and I will ever see. Almost a feeling of cheerfulness, of happiness among the few unadorned Graves, where red Poppies alone break the cream-white of Portland stones. All huddled up together, in Life and Death!

I see Craiglockhart, nurses with large hats, the high ceilings, Siegfried Sassoon, that short Summer of my Life, I was happy there. I was teaching, writing. I found myself there. Mother, where has my Life gone?' [4.8.17]

159.Stuck in the Past

As I start the regression, Wilfred is here and sits in my chair, in uniform and hat. I feel his sadness as he becomes me. There is a great expansion of the heart chakra as painful memories flood in. I am overwhelmed.

'I see the Canal stretching out in front of me. How strange to be here again, walking on the green grass with my laced shoes, uniform and hat. I am alone!

I see trenches, muddy roads and fields, stunted trees, corpses laying here and there, glass-eyed faces frozen in death, legs asunder, arms spread out like Crosses; ragged Uniforms splattered with blood. The Horror of it all! Will it ever leave me?

I walk through the muddy field, stepping over the bodies that lie at my feet. I feel intense pain. I cannot let go. The Futility of it all!'

Wilfred sits in my chair, tears running down his cheeks, head bent, chin touching his chest.

'I cannot let go. I carry the pain of all my Soldiers, they cling to me, we are all One' he says, suddenly subdued.

Susan Owen: Life without Wilfred

'I see Susan Owen in her 40s [?] still an attractive woman. She cannot accept having outlived her son- though she would never admit this. Her life is now a life of resignation and sadness, of memories and times gone by. She longs to be united with her son, but her life will be long and Wilfred will not be there to meet her, he is still where he fell, in that small Cemetery where Sons and Daughters, Fathers and Mothers lie together. There is no sadness there. The sadness is on the Battlefield where all your Hopes and Dreams died.' [7.8.17]

160.A 'Gay' Question

As I start the regression, Wilfred is here in my chair. I feel uneasy as something stirs in my heart, and wants to come up, but cannot. What is still upsetting you, Wilfred, what do you regret most? I ask. How did you feel when you were sent back to the Battlefield?

'Like a Lamb to Slaughter. I knew I would die, most of Us did, but I did not tell my Mother.' Wilfred's face is tense with emotion, unexpressed pain. He stares calmly into Infinity. Where you ready to die? I ask.

'Though I accepted Death, I was not really ready to go, so much to live for...None of Us really was. I am joined by my Friends, now, they are all around me' he says. I see Susan Owen, long gown with apron, her face sad and serious. Were you gay, Wilfred?

'No, I was not 'gay' he replies with the lightest impression of a smile. 'I was shy of girls and more comfortable with young men of my age, but was not 'gay' as you put it. I did not live long enough to experience women and my poetry and work brought me close mostly to men with ambitions as my own.' he adds.

I start crying and he cries with me. [8.8.17]

161.Craiglockhart

A long, rambling regression all bits and pieces.

'I see a young Wilfred, wearing a white coat, like a doctor. Strange, I have never seen him like that before. His hair is parted in the middle of his young, beautiful face. I feel sad and want to cry. I see a big house with big arches behind him-Craiglockhart?' [9.8.17]

162.The Canal again

I see shoes with laces, 'bandaged' legs. I am wearing a long jacket and belt, round hat. Wilfred is here, sitting in my chair. I sink into the essence of his being. Wilfred, what are your thoughts?

'The Canal appears in front of me. I crush the green grass with my heavy shoes. No-one is here. I walk alone, lost in my thoughts.'

An Act of Kindness

I now see Wilfred superimposed on Albert. Suddenly, unexpectedly, he bends down and whispers something very personal to me in my ear, and not about himself, as I prepare to close the regression. 'Never give up in the face of Adversity' he says, his face close to mine, I can feel the warmth of his breath. How appropriate. He knows what I am going through. Never before a former Personality stepped out of its confines to comfort and advise me. I am blown away. Thank you, Wilfred! [10.8.17]

163.A New Man

As usual, Wilfred is sitting in my chair, in uniform, no hat. He looks young, but weary.

'I see the Canal, a picture of peace, so different from what we knew then' he says. He stares into Infinity with great sadness and I feel pain in my solar plexus. I see Wilfred as an 18-year-old, with puppy face, a picture of honesty and integrity.

'Those Dream Days' he sighs 'and the Harsh Reality. Mother brought us up well, deep into her religious principles. They bound and limited me throughout my short life' he pauses. 'She was my lifeblood in my Darkest Hour, but did I believe them in the End?' Please let go, Wilfred, I ask, for your own sake and mine. I see Craiglockhart and its patients in the grounds.

'I went there shell-shocked, my Life in ruin, shattered

Beliefs. I emerged a new Man, Free' he sighs. Did you enjoy being there?

'Yes. From the cracked chrysalid of my Life I emerged a new Man and truly Lived. Craiglockhart made me. When I went to the Front, part of me was already dead, though I was very much alive, the slate wiped clean, but there would be no new beginnings' he says, lost in thoughts. 'I accepted Death and the fact that I would almost certainly die. I felt exhilaratingly free of all Beliefs and Limitations, and focused on my Soldiers and care for them as much as I could.

I had no time to think. The ground was covered with bodies, the blood was flowing, men were falling like flies. The air was thick with smoke and the deafening sound of mortar over our heads. It was Hell. Valour? Medals? What use are they to me now?' he asks with bitterness in his voice 'I simply cared for my Soldiers and tried to protect them. They were my world and still are.' [12.8.17]

168.Stuck in the Past

This is a very difficult Past Life to clear, because of the complexity of feelings and the depth of the trauma suffered as a Soldier fighting a War, something which affects all Soldiers, in various degrees, after which their lives will never be the same again. Wilfred Owen has come to represent for me the suffering of Soldiers of all Times and, as such, parts of his Soul will remain anchored to the Earth Plane leaving his Soul incomplete and unfulfilled, until something happens, however long into the future, to unblock them, like the end of all Wars and a new Era of Peace for the Earth.

'I sit in my chair in World War One uniform, but do not know who I am yet. I see the dark silhouettes of Soldiers against a livid sky. Stunted trees and scorched earth around them, mud everywhere, bodies half buried in it. I see one Soldier, his glazed eyes staring vacantly into the sky. What a sight! What a waste! What Youth denied!

I see a 17/18-year-old Wilfred, clean-faced, innocent

looking, his Soul still whole, still unravaged by the experience of War.

I see modern-day Soldiers and ask them to leave, but they are reluctant, they have their own Stories to tell. I feel for them too, but I focus on Wilfred. Fragments of other Souls are attached to him and hold him back and hold themselves back.

I ask Wilfred if he wants to say something, he has been very quiet. I am getting tired and want to go.

A young/old Wilfred stares in front of himself, lost in thoughts, tormented, cannot find peace. I cannot force him to speak. I feel pain in my heart. 'Let go, let go, Wilfred' I say.

Susan Owen: Death of A Son

Suddenly, I see an older woman, perhaps in her late 40s early 50s, her hair combed back but dishevelled, wearing a long skirt and apron. I do not recognise her, though I see her very clearly. She is distressed. Susan Owen? It looks as if she is in a farmhouse, but I only see a tiny corner of it. I do not know her. She now wears lovely [Victorian?] clothes, lovely shirt and jacket, hat - Susan?' She sits in my chair, hat, jacket, all. 'Do you want to say something, Susan?' I ask. I feel her pain, deep, deep, deep down.

'The day Wilfred died the Light went out for me' she says softly. 'I died with him that Day.' [19.8.17]

169.Always by My Side

Last night I felt a terrible sorrow in my heart relating to a Past Life and decided to do a regression to find out what it was.

'I sink deeper and deeper into the Well of Time and Wilfred slowly emerges in uniform and a hat. I feel pain in my solar plexus. I feel it, let it grow and expand. I am totally immersed in it. Feel the pain and let go.

176.Craiglockhart-Happy Moments

'I start the regression and after a while Wilfred appears against a background of Soldiers' silhouettes against a livid sky.

I see Craiglockhart[119] and its large grounds and its patients, Wilfred looking the young man that he is. I see him engaging in various activities and enjoying some normality in his life. I go back a few years and see a teenage Wilfred posing for a photograph with his happy Family in front of a beautiful home.'

How can I help you, Wilfred? I ask, but there is no reply.

180.Images of War

I have been waking up at nights with bouts of anxiety and I know there is a Past Life which wants to come up. Wilfred, is that you? A rather indistinct form appears Out of the Mists of Time, Wilfred Owen. He stands behind me, his hands on my shoulders. Suddenly, I am him and he sits in this chair, writing this account.

Wilfred, what can I do to help you? I ask and suddenly cry. There is always such a heavy load of responsibility, of disappointment, with Wilfred that at times it is overwhelming.

I see the Sambre-Oise Canal, a Battlefield, devastation and desolation, bodies: these are haunting images which will not leave him and regularly come up in regression.

Can you describe the moment you were hit and died? I ask. I feel the pain rising from the solar plexus and a wave of emotion engulfing me. What happened, Wilfred? I do not want to put words in his mouth, there is a strong resistance to let go.

'I saw Death, riding over the Battlefield, Soldiers falling like Flies, the sounds of explosions, Hell broken loose, there was no Salvation, no Escape for Us. We were doomed from the start. What a useless War!'

There is great bitterness in Wilfred's heart.

'We were all caught up in a Game of Greed, false Ambitions, Death, and Destruction. How can we Atone for the Millions who died?'

A Spokesman for all Soldiers

Wilfred stands alone on a vast pit of nameless bones, truly Universal, removed from the trappings of Humanity. He truly feels for all Soldiers. He represents their sorrow and their longing for Happiness and the despair of their unfulfilled Lives. How can I help him in this, how can I release your Soul? There seems to be no easy way. My body contracts in a strong spasm. I urge Wilfred to speak. I want to close the session. I am tired as a lot of my energy has gone into this.

Regrets

'The Futility of War!

It robbed me of my Innocence and Faith!' he adds with bitterness. 'What would my Life had been, had I lived?'

But you did not, Wilfred, so let it go, I say, and be at Peace. But there is no Peace for the Fallen. [24.9.17]

192.The Last Rising Day

I went to a concert in memory of Wilfred Owen recently and was moved by the organizers' commitment to keep his memory alive. His Nephew was there and it was a privilege to be in his company. I felt deep affection for him, he looked very much like Wilfred, especially the eyes and I felt the connection with him. Wilfred is now sitting in my chair and writing this. He is in uniform, wearing his hat.

'I see the rise of a new day on the Sambre-Oise Canal. I see trenches and Soldiers 'burrowed' in them. For many the rise of the New Day will be their last.' [27.1.18]

193.What Would I Have Been Had I Lived?

I am sitting in my garden having a cup of coffee in a lovely China cup with Wilfred's photograph on it. It is a beautiful sunny morning. He is sitting in my place, in uniform and hat. It is good to be able to glide through Lives and Time, is it not, Wilfred? I ask. He is enjoying the sunshine, the small garden, clothes on the line to dry. It is a peaceful moment for him.

'I wished I lived longer!' he suddenly whispers, lost in thoughts. I see him dressed in civilian clothes, hair parted in the middle, a young intellectual, thin moustache, pale- blue eyes. 'I feel short-changed by Life' he adds after a pause, with bitterness in his voice. 'I live in you, but this does not compensate for my losses in my Life.'

Thank you, Wilfred, I say. Look at those deep-red roses bending down towards you-the colour of your Soldiers' blood. Are they really lost forever? Every year I cut them down and they come back stronger and stronger, and so do we. 'Yes, but the opportunities offered by that Life are gone forever, or maybe until such time as they will present themselves again, but not to me as I was then' he says after a long pause. 'Be as it may, that Life was incomplete because of those losses, and that I deeply regret. I live Life through you, but that is not the same as living that Life myself, as I was then. That 'me' is gone forever and cannot come back.' Suddenly he is silent and lost in thoughts.

'An unfulfilled Life, an unfulfilled Promise. Did I make a mark on Life? Perhaps I did. But what is that to me now?' he asks, looking at me with bitterness. I cannot reply, I am upset as he is. I wish I could help him find peace. The red roses are resplendent in the sunshine, cut against a blue sky. Many are fading, others are falling, new blooms are emerging-the cycle of Life. As I prepare to close the session, Wilfred speaks again. 'Perhaps I was not meant to live long. If so, I fulfilled my Destiny and I am fulfilled. I can see now, I was meant to speak of the horrors of War, to de-glamourize War, but at what price!' [10.6.18]

A Welcome Visit

I was having a cup of coffee in the garden, when suddenly Wilfred appeared. I placed a chair by my side, so he could sit by me. It is a lovely morning and the sun is shining and the red roses are out in their glory. It is a bit windy, but it is pleasant. This is an unexpected visit which gives me pleasure. I love his presence.

Wilfred is in uniform and hat, boots, and he is beautiful, just like the young man that he once was. I am going through a difficult time and he knows it. That is why he is here. His presence is a great comfort to me. He is the only Incarnation that stepped out of the limitations of the Past into the Present to care for me. It is remarkable and unique, nothing ever happened to me like this before. We are One, so we both benefit from this. Wilfred has now taken over, I have disappeared, and he is writing this. The wind is blowing the red roses with its gentle breath, we hear its voice, the air is pregnant with their delicious scent, everything moves and is alive. There is perfect harmony just now.

'I love your little garden' - Wilfred whispers. A small red rose has just opened and stands alone, aside from the others. It is exquisite in shape and colour and is kissed by the sun. It is full of beauty and promise. Others are in full bloom, their colour heightened by the sun, others in the shadow, blood red. Some are fading, their petals scattered by the wind. 'Just like us' -he says thoughtfully - 'We were blown by the Wind of War, our Remains scattered over the Battlefield'. There is great sadness, and a new acceptance, he has moved on or is moving on. At last. A welcome development. [He is writing this, but I am just now speaking through him.]

'My boots weigh heavily on my feet, but I am comfortable with my Uniform. I am happy and grateful that I can still experience Life through you, breathe the air you breathe and see your world as a Person, rather than a Discarnate Spirit. You give me this opportunity. You make me live again - he blurts out suddenly, with enthusiasm - and I am young again. Priceless!' His eyes are shining with a new Light, a new Energy, a beautiful young man, the Ugliness and Brutality of the War behind him. Will this last? Will he move on towards the Light and leave the Earth Plane?

We were interrupted by a telephone call, but Wilfred is still here, thoughtful, gazing the roses in silence. Do you miss Life? - I ask, and realise what a silly question it is. 'I miss my Life <u>then</u>'- he whispers, but without pain. The wind is too strong now, and I am going in. [10.5.20]

Chapter 19

World War Two[12] [1939-1945]

38.A Close Call

'I WAS SOMEWHERE, war time, with a German Soldier.

They were leading us to some place and dividing us in two groups. I was close to this Soldier and asked him if he had children. He looked at me and took me out of one group and put me in the other. That moment I knew he had saved my life.

I was a Soldier, too.' [27.11.00]

62.A German Firing Squad

'I saw a beautiful young Soldier, perhaps early 20s, with very fine features like those of a woman, so beautiful he was. He had short, brown, wavy, hair parted on the side, finely chiselled nose and mouth, beautiful eyes. A small delicate face. He was in uniform. I saw German Soldiers and thought it was World War One, but more likely World War Two, and think he was Polish.

I saw a battlefield, trenches; an execution. His hands tied behind his back, against a wall, a German firing squad. I saw his face, dead, amongst others. What a sight!'

I was overcome with emotion. The pain, the horror of what I witnessed hit me in the stomach with tremendous force. I asked him to meet the Germans who shot him.

'There he was, with others shot with him, very angry, shouting at the Germans who had emerged from the mists of Time and were reluctant to come forward. Eventually, they spoke in very low voice and said they also were Soldiers who executed their orders, just like their victims had done'.

I told them there were no victors, they were all losers. I asked them to forgive One Another, leave their Graves and the Earth Plane and their attachments to my energy field, move on to Higher Realms and be at Peace.

'I was that Polish Soldier.' [22.7.13]

182.The Red Army in the Snow

I have been feeling increasingly anxious since I returned from my Pilgrimage to various Concentration Camps. Something important is surfacing to consciousness.

'This morning, during a short meditation, I suddenly saw a vast expanse of frozen land covered with snow, with dried bushes here and there.

I saw Soldiers with rifles on their backs, wearing long coats, tight from shoulders to the waist, with belts, boots, fur caps with a golden star [the Red Army] advancing in the snow. I was one of them. I am wearing that uniform and fur cap over my ears and most of my face, as I write this.' Something 'bubbled' up from my throat chakra - a release. [6.11.17]

The Katyn Massacre[26] [1940]

19.Defending Polish Skies

'There were some Officers, one sitting without a jacket, some of them young men, and some Russian Soldiers with long coats and hats with flaps on their ears, with bayonets. I saw General Bohatyrewicz[8] and Colonel Pawlikowski[8] and wrote them a letter.' [9.7.97]

48.An Orgy of Killings

This is a very long, very distressing and detailed Life in World War II which, with other unhappy Lives as a Soldier, has created a pattern of lasting depression, sorrow, anxiety, and unhappiness which needs to be cleared to break the Karmic cycle. It brought up many strong feelings and left me exhausted and extremely upset for many weeks.

'I saw a young Officer with a soft face and sad thoughtful eyes. I was that Man. I wear uniform, beret, a long jacket with collar and belt, trousers, fine leather boots. I am an Officer, a Polish Officer.

The Beginning of The End

Reaching concentration camp, trucks full of Soldiers. There is a dormitory in the camp, looks like an old faded photograph. An Officer in a long, shabby coat stands outside the dormitory smoking a cigarette, the sun shining in his eyes. I see faces of men, round hats, the dormitory- part brick/part wood. I see the shape of a door, a rectangular, dark space, a dormitory, rocks outside.

There is a man in a collared uniform with small metal stars on each side of the collar, with a round hat, wearing boots, belt, an officer, in front of me. He is Russian. I feel very hot inside, very angry, but do not feel hatred. He tells Polish Officers of this Regiment where they will go, about their being taken to a camp and then sent back to Poland. A lot of lies, never told the truth, they treat us well. They know what they will do with us, but will not tell us, to keep us quiet/happy, they deceive us.

I speak with a different voice, someone has come through, low, raucous voice with a tinge of despair in it. I am Commanding Officer of this Regiment, a Regiment of Officers, the Elite of the Army. I have no choice about commanding them, do what they tell you. We are prisoners, nothing we can do, but do as we are told!

'Going Home'

I see some men, a Polish Officer on right side, somebody else, many military trucks, Soldiers marching, disarmed prisoners, many loaded into trucks like cattle, transported somewhere. It is a sunny day, long coats worn out, really messy, messy, very foggy, could be winter. I see the Forest from above, looking down, very foggy and grey, only seen the top of the bare branches, no leaves on trees. Trucks are driving among trees, barely able to go through, very strange. It is winter, no leaves on trees.

I see a Russian soldier, blue eyes, another soldier like me. Snow around as well, very dismal place, depressing, gloomy, squalid. Prisoners are unloaded from their trucks, a Russian soldier, belt, rifle, big moustache, supervising – whatever happens, happens quickly.

Looking down from higher up, I see treetops, no leaves, very foggy and grey-some are-the forest-space-no trees. I see a dark big hole in a wide, open space in the middle of this Forest, a deep open wound in the earth, big, dark. I see the bodies of the Soldiers, a mass Grave, a large rectangular hole freshly dug up, roots sticking out of the soil like broken teeth, the Soldiers looking at me with glassy eyes. Strange view. I feel very sick.

Happier Times

I have seen a photograph of myself in uniform, leather boots, jacket, pockets, collar, belt, black wavy hair, Proust-like face, before going to war. I see vague images of Warsaw[27] where I was born and where I grew up. I live in Warsaw, a big town, beautiful. I am very happy. I see my town, buildings, university, people in the streets. I am an architect. I built several buildings, one of them with steeples, quite tall, stone building, of which I am proud.

I see a young beautiful blonde woman with corsetand slim gown [possibly before 1900]. See one boy, blond hair with trousers and chemise like a Victorian boy [that style of clothes]; also, two beautiful blonde girls, all aged 11-12 years perhaps. Seen a photo of a woman [toponly] dressed in black, black hair Victorian style, but Polish, about 40 years old, hair done up, perhaps my Mother.

I have a young wife who calls me 'Nisha' or 'Misha', Russian short for Michael. We have a daughter, perhaps 8/10 years old, and a boy. I love them. We live very comfortably in a large, beautiful home, like a Victorian house, in Warsaw, we do have servants. We go out a lot, go to theatre a lot - not very big, but beautiful, balcony.

Look down on stage, on actors, stone building in town, house in town, studied here, grew up here. I met my wife at the University where we studied. Of the University, I only see an open window.

My name is Adrian Wojciech Moszynski.

The Dream Is Over

I now see what looks like a rectangular hut, long, made of bricks or wood, perhaps a dormitory, all very hazy. I see only the faint outlines, like a faded photograph, but bright, not dark. A man with a round military hat and long shabby coat, good-looking and young, maybe 30 years old, in front of the hut/dormitory, obviously winter, but sunny. Do not know who he is, perhaps an inmate, a prisoner, or a Russian soldier [no rifle though]. Heseems kind and cheerful [strange]. A Polish officer drops in this picture and he is on my right-hand side. He is young, perhaps 30 years old, with pale blue eyes, looking a bit like the actor playing James Bond now.

A Russian soldier with a felt triangular hat, long coat with belt, blue-grey in colour, pale blue eyes, big moustache, long rifle, appears. 'Bloody Russian!' I blurt out in a fit of emotion, then I am sorry, 'he is just another Soldier like me, he does what he is told to do. He is not responsible for what is happening'.

Snow… Very dismal place, depressing, gloomy, grey, squalid [the Forest in winter]. I cry unexpectedly. I ask what happens next and how I die. I describe what I see.

It is all foggy and grey and I do not know. I do not see family and friends, I see nothing, only rarefied air and thick clouds like the ones we traverse when flying on a plane. I see the Forest, the bare trees, the big dark hole [mass Grave] like a deep wound.

BANG, BANG, BANG!'

A Russian general quickly walks behind kneeling Officers, their hands tied up behind their backs, and quickly shoots them in the nape of the head, kicking them with his foot into the grave they previously dug up. Death is quick. I burst into tears again, unexpectedly and surprised at this show of emotion.

I ask myself: How do I feel about my life and my Comrades' lives, ending like that? A waste, a total waste. I could have lived like others, a family, friends, work, a bourgeois life.

I was only 46 years old when I died.'

49.A Release

'I saw the top of the barren trees, the clearing in the middle and the large, dark rectangular hole, the mass Grave. I saw the bodies of the Soldiers covered in blood, one on top of the other. I brought some Light into the Grave and saw these pale, white, thin, ethereal Bodies and Souls lifting, leaving their Graves and reaching out, high up in the sky towards the Light and into the Light. The Grave was filled with dark- red rose petals falling from the sky and then with white petals. As the Grave was filled with fresh Soil, beautiful white lilies sprang up towards the Light.

Let tears of joy and rejuvenation replace tears of trauma and suffering. Let tears of reconciliation wash away tears of frustration and anger and let there be peace.' [13.5.13]

51.Another Polish Life Another Death

'In 1939-40 I was a Polish Soldier in Russia. My name was Tadeus Makiovich. Apparently, the prisoners from Ostashkhov[28] were drowned and those who did not were shot in the water.' [6.6.13]

76.Visions

Before I started a one-hour regression, Padre Pio and Mother Theresa came to me. I also saw a man dressed in white, with white turban, young, with a very black short beard and moustache. He was with me for a considerable time [a Spiritual Guide?].

'I saw the dark, rectangular, Grave at Katyn, trees without leaves around it. Went down that large black hole until there was no light penetrating it. It seemed empty. I felt empty, with little pain. I saw a Russian Soldier with small triangular cap and long coat; then I saw another Soldier, with fur cap and long coat and boots, square face, not unpleasant. I felt I could be that Soldier. I saw a winter landscape with snow and Russian Soldiers with bayonets on the attack, trees behind them, open space in front. I saw Hussars[49], but thought it was an interference.' Did not get details of a life, and did not feel severe pain, only a little. [12.8.13]

79.The Forest Then and Now

Did two-hour long regression. Confused images at first, but then things cleared up.

'First, I saw the Western Desert, then Katyn, the black rectangular hole [the mass Grave], trees covered with leaves and a Russian Soldier with long winter coat, boots and beret with ear flaps folded up. I also saw Katyn Forest.[52] as it is today.' Very sad, and very upsetting, Memories.

144.A Sad memory-The Mass Grave

'I saw the black rectangular hole [the mass Grave], trees covered with leaves and a Russian Soldier with long winter coat, boots and beret with ear flaps folded up.

El Alamein North Africa[34,50] [1942]

23.A Plane Crash

A great wave of sadness came over me as I briefly recalled this Life. 'I saw an Officer in uniform and boots, very good-looking, very, very blond, with a very white and beautiful skin, and then a wreckage of a plane with a body in it in military clothes, blond hair, very pale.' Oh, how my heart aches!

30.An Honourable Man: Rommel

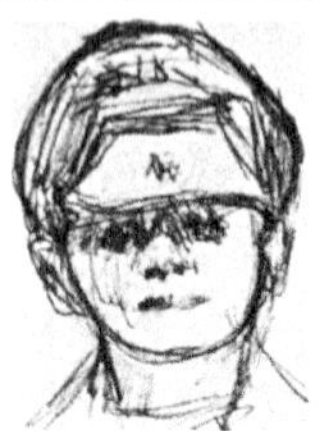

'I saw myself when I was about 3 years old. Rommel[9] lifts me up and holds me. He was an inspiration to me. I was a child and knew him. I did not have a long life, but he was kind to me and I loved him. He was a good friend of my mother's and she loved him too. He impressed me with his tales and visionary skills. He entertained me with stories of magic and knights and quests and romances. My family were not Nazis and not against them. They knew Rommel as a friend and the Nazi Party just came along as a political entity which did not bother or over- excite my family.' [7.4.99]

32.The Aviator

'I saw an Aviator with cap and long ear flaps, wearing a cream-white overall, his face a bit like young Prince Philip's. He was standing by a plane and the sun shone in his eyes–good-looking, tall. I was that Aviator.' [19.7.99]

45.RAF Bomber Pilot

'An RAF Bomber Pilot in North Africa whose plane was shot down in the desert, came up a few times, but no details.'

56.The Cemeteries

There is a lot of emotion and pain associated with this Life. [1.7.13]

'Saw the Cross and slowly went back to El Alamein[34], to the Cemeteries, the Italian and German Cemeteries.'

I saw the white gravestones[35] emerging from the beautiful red, dry, and powdery soil, under the intense blue sky in the burning sunshine, forever there. I was overcome with emotion. I also saw an Arab Sheik with moustache and beard and felt I was him.

68. RAF Pilot

I started a regression, but could not proceed as I suddenly felt very tired and laid down with a bad headache, the muscles of my legs and my whole body very painful and heavy, like lead, as my blood pressure went down. They were the physical memories, shockwaves of a sudden, violent death, which lasted several hours. I had stumbled on a major Past Life of which I caught a glim pse. 'I saw an RAF pilot in blue overall, like a car mechanic, and felt I was him as I am still now as I write.' I still felt awful, headache, stomach churned up. Went back to bed. [24.7.13]

78.Death in the Desert

Then I saw El Alamein Cemetery, the Battlefield, the Desert.' I have always felt very emotional about El Alamein[50]and did not know why. The mention of that name was enough to make me cry. I always wanted to go there, and I did.

'I was a young Bomber Pilot by the side of my plane, and was wearing short trousers, a sleeveless, open-neck, shirt, heavy shoes with laces, knee- long thick socks, and looked relaxed. Tall and attractive, 22 years old, blond wavy short hair, parted on the left side, Australian looking, but in fact, Irish. I saw the Desert, and suddenly he was me, sitting on my sofa and crying. He cried for a long time with his head in his hands.

There were some English Soldiers, someone very high-up the line[51] round hat, square face, thin moustache, British and German Soldiers, tanks rolling in the Desert raising clouds of sand; Rommel very briefly, fighting going on, planes bombing enemy lines.

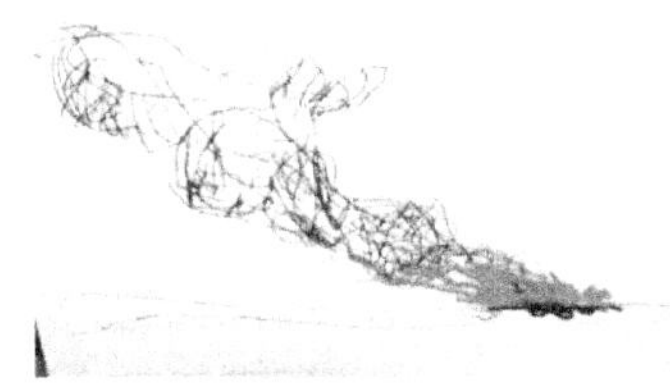

I was in the cockpit of a plane, when the plane was shot down and blew up in a fireball. I saw the blaze of the fire outside the cockpit as I raised my hands and then nothing but darkness and death.' What was the last thought?

'There was no time to think'

Sitting on the sofa as the Pilot, I asked myself if I had wished for something and after a pause, I thought: 'I wish I had more time.'

'I went back to the crash scene and the darkness [the death scene] and then I saw the young Pilot, short trousers, going up towards a very strong, round shaped White Light. As the Pilot went up, I was above Him and looked down on Him, he was looking up towards the bright White Light, his arms close to his body, like Superman, going up towards and into the very beautiful strong silvery White Light, as I released Him.' [10.8.13]

146.Montgomery-Airmen

Suddenly, I see Montgomery, Airmen in their smart blue uniforms, planes in the sky, a Pilot in a cockpit, and a group of Airmen in front of a plane posing for a photograph.

171.Rommel: A Sudden Death [14 October 1944]

'Quite unexpectedly, Rommel appears.

I see him surveying his position in the Desert. My parents knew him well and I loved him in that Life. He is lost in thought. I see him in that car, on that fateful day, his wife on the doorstep, while he was driven away. I feel pain in my heart, sadness, bitterness.

I was given a capsule. I took it and was dead within seconds' he says 'it was that quick. I was catapulted out of my body and found myself looking down from somewhere higher up, my body slumped in the back seat, the car speeding up. I was confused, did not understand what was happening, why was I high up looking down? I did not realise I was dead. It was all new to me' he adds. What was your last thought? I ask him.

'While the car drove off from my home, my thoughts were in turmoil, my heart full of contrasting emotions, but I was calm. I had seen Death many times before and now it was happening to me. It all ended soon after we left my house. There was no time to think, but bitterness and regret' Rommel concludes with a sigh. What regret? I ask, surprised. I feel pain and a heavy heart.

'That the Plot failed' he whispers. [23.8.17]

177.Death in the Desert

I was feeling restless and upset for no apparent reason all week so I decided to investigate.

'At the start of the regression, El Alamein came through with an image of the Desert and an Officer covered with sand. There is a sandstorm and this Soldier is lost in it.' My heart chakra is very heavy. 'He is a British Officer, tall, blond. The sky is covered with whirlwind sand, there is no visibility, no protection from the storm, from the sand which fills his hair, eyes, lungs, and makes it impossible to breathe. What a terrible way to die!' I am devastated. 'He falls to the ground, his body quickly buried in the sand, his eyes half-open, one last painful gasp, one last breath, before choking to death.'

I try to get one last thought. I feel his despair, his fear. Who are you? I ask, not really expecting a reply. I feel great pain and a strong pull on the solar plexus, something trying to come up. What happened to you?

'I was on a reconnaissance mission, but lost my way, the plane ran out of fuel. I knew I would die. I was miles away from anything, but I stepped out of the plane in the vain hope that a miracle would happen to save myself, but it did not' he adds with bitterness. I suddenly feel very emotional and cry. I am overwhelmed by the intensity of his feelings. 'I did not go very far. A sandstorm suddenly overtook me. I tried to run from it, in vain. My strength was failing and I collapsed, engulfed by sand. The Desert became my grave as I disappeared quickly, gasping for breath.' What was your last thought? I ask.

I see his short, wavy, blond hair, parted on the left side, a young, intelligent, face.

'I was only twenty-two years old and expected more from Life than this' he whispers. [2.9.17]

178.Death in the Desert Part II

I feel tension in my heart, something is trying to manifest itself into consciousness. I feel pain slowly filling my chest. I take a deep breath. I see the vast expansion of the Desert in its solitary glory. There is nothing there. A flat expansion of nothingness where one can see for miles and everything is very exposed. There is peace in all this. I levitate over a sea of golden sand. Where am I going? I take another deep breath. I am very close to the sand, but I am not touching it, like a plane skimming the runway before landing. I immerse myself in my solar plexus to discover this hidden reality.

'I see this Man lying flat on the sand, his hands close to

his face, his face very close to mine. There is loneliness and despair in his Soul. I feel the impact of this emotion in my heart, it is overpowering. The sky is now clear, the sandstorm has abated, all is silent and peaceful. I ask him to show me parts of his Life. I see him in uniform, tall, wavy, blond, hair parted on the left, in a group, but I do not see others in this group, only him. I try to sketch his likeness, but it is very difficult. He has a full face, good features, wavy, blond hair. I think he is the same man I saw yesterday.'

I end the regression because I get confused information, as if from two Past Lives, like 'being from Ireland', 'lance corporal'; uniform with bandaged; legs as if from World War One rather than World War Two/. [14.9.17]

194.German Soldiers

For the last few months, a Past Life has tried to surface, creating great discomfort and anxiety, mostly at night, and feelings of overwhelming fear which I have tried to ignore, but they are getting much worse and I decided to try a regression.

'I see German Soldiers, with their helmets, Nazi Soldiers, actually, I see one in particular.' I have a heavy solar plexus, something is stirring deep down, with great pain.

Rommel

'I see German Soldiers in action, it is quite dark, early morning/late afternoon. I see a German Officer by profile, quite tall, long coat, boots, round hat, top brass. Do not see him well, looks a bit like Rommel. It is Rommel, the sun in his eyes, staring ahead of him. It is the Desert, Rommel surveying the open spaces in front of him with binoculars, lost in thoughts. The sun is high in the sky, ahead of a long column of motorized vehicles andtanks.' I feel pain in my stomach-very uneasy.

'I see German Soldiers again. I am one of them, sitting at my desk wearing uniform and helmet, writing this. I have a heavy heart. I see another Soldier, young, wearing 'wide' trousers at the top, knee-long boots, short, tight- fitting jacket with waist belt, small hat. I do not know who he is.' Various confusing images. It is late, I am getting bored and I stop. No doubt the anxiety will still be there in the morning, for days to come. [11.12.18]

Reflections

Something remarkable happened tonight while I was watching New Year's Eve celebrations on TV. I began to feel sad and anxious for no particular reason which lasted for some time and got progressively worse, until something stirred up from deep inside me and someone inside me said out aloud 'Oh, I am very, very unhappy!' a few times. I was so surprised! I did not speak those words. Someone else did, from inside me, from the mists of Time, from the Past, quite distinct from myself. I had to discover who it was. [31.12.18]

Battle Of Normandy [1944]

24.A Flashback: An Aviator

'I saw a man, an aviator, wearing an aviator's cap, shirt and trousers, but no jacket; dark hair and a couple of deep lines in his forehead, black eyes and thick moustache, vaguely looked like the actor Clark Gable. He was in his late forties, early fifties.' [11.9.98]

184.US Army-Normandy Landings[110]

I continue to be tense, so I try a regression. I feel pain in my solar plexus and in my chest, very intense. I do not know what causes it. It must be a very painful Past Life.

My maternal Grandfather and my Mother are here with me and protect me. I feel a spasm of anxiety in my chest as I start.

A Marine

'I see Battlefields, Soldiers attacking. They are Marines! I see their helmets, their rifles, their boots, as they run on the attack. I see tanks rolling forward, sinking into the mud. There is this Marine in front of me. He is in the shadow. I do not see his face. His uniform is stained with mud. He holds a carbine[109] like a baby, close to his heart. I see his face now, by profile. He is a young man, under thirty. A good, American face, attractive, good features.

I see a long beach, thousands and thousands of Marines jumping off their boats, wading through water, their carbines high on their shoulders, tanks disembarking from their carriers. There is such frenzied activity, the momentum is building up to fever pitch. I cry with intense emotion. All these brave men!

An All-American Town

The Soldiers disembark, in huge numbers, like black masses of swarming ants. I cry again, the emotion is too strong. What happened to the Marine? Who was him? I lost him now. A face in the crowd. Suddenly, I see a peaceful, prosperous, quintessentially American town of low buildings, bungalows, with large garden lawns in front of them, neatly arranged on a slight hill with trees, gently sloping down1 to a large main avenue. There is a young man, perhaps twenty years old, tall, blond with a striking face, good looking, a student, holding books, looking happy. The Future is rosy with anticipation. So much to live for! His parents have great expectations for him. How their hopes will be shattered!

Going Home in a Box

I see coffins covered with the Flag with the Stars slowly descending from the belly of a large, heavy plane, carried by Soldiers. I feel immensely sad, upset. The sun shines high in the sky. I see the face of this young Soldier. I feel his disappointment. He stares vacantly in front of him.' [14.1.18]

186.US Marine-A Grisly End

'I see Soldiers' silhouettes on the horizon against a livid sky. I see this Marine opposite me wearing a helmet, sun in his eyes. He is the same Soldier I saw two days ago. He is me and I am him, we are one and the same as I sit in my chair in uniform and helmet. There is sadness in his eyes as he stares in front of him. His face reminds me of the 1950s singer Pat Boone, only more good looking. I see this prosperous American town with neat, orderly homes like bungalows and trees on a low hill, and the main avenue. There is a happy feeling there. Suddenly, I feel upset as I sit in my chair, my head reclined on my chest. Who am I? What happened to me? How did I die?

I see a shell hitting my chest and blasting me to pieces. It was a split second as my body parts flew in all directions. A grisly end.' What was the last thought?

'There was no time to think. I was ejected from my body suddenly, with great speed, in a stupor, and for a long time did not know what had happened to me. I just stood there among the debris of War, unable to think, to comprehend what was going on. I could not see my body. I thought I was still alive. I joined other Soldiers, fighting, but they did not see me. The truth finally dawned on me: I was dead and it was hard to accept. I was traumatized by the discovery that I was dead. This memory still gives me great pain. I was desperate, I did not know what to do. I hung around and saw others killed. Suddenly, I saw my home town in 1950s America, my parents, my Father, thinner hair on his forehead, wearing glasses, and my Mother, hair combed back, both in their mid-fifties. I felt their anxiety for me. I felt sorry for the Sorrow I caused them'. What happened next? I ask myself still sitting in uniform and helmet.

'It was the thought of their love that saved me, as a Shaft of White Light suddenly appeared in front of me and I walked through it and disappeared.' [16.1.18]

Another Marine

In the last few months, I have been troubled by very high blood pressure from tension and anxiety and I decided to investigate a possible Past Life connection.

'There is a Soldier, a Marine, on a beach holding a rifle, next to a barbed wire spike. He is looking in the distance and appears to be alone. He is the Marine who looks like the Singer Pat Boone, attractive. He looks worried. I am slowly turning into that Marine, with his fears and anxiety as I sink into myself. There is pain in the solar plexus and I dive into it, like a black monster with a cavernous mouth, the deeper you go, the further you go, seems endless. A lot of resistance makes that Life difficult to access. I cannot go deep enough and end the session. [28.5.20]

195.A Soldier

In the last few months, I have had moments of great anxiety, mostly at night, of growing distress, and last night was a particularly bad one. I could hardly breathe and feared a full-scale panic attack. I managed to relax and fend it off, but I know there is something BIG which needs to be brought to light. Today I have decided to try with a regression.

A very intense feeling is slowly being released from the solar plexus, as I start the Regression and take a deep, long, breath. I enter the solar plexus and begin to move around a deep-seated pain. I take a deep breath to bringit up, but there is strong resistance. I take another breath and dig deep into it. I walk into the darkness of this pain and, suddenly, a Face dimly appears. A young Man, with brown hair, slightly curly, long chin, a narrow Face, thin moustache-good looking. I go further into the Darkness. He is still with me - can only see the Face, a young Man with delicate features and a sensitive, intelligent, Face. I begin the feel the Pain, feel the Pain and let go. It is releasing slowly, with great difficulty. I do not know what this Pain is about, but it is intense. I tried for about an hour, but could not go deep enough, and ended the session. [23.1.19]

196.A German Teenage Soldier

I decided to try again, because the pain and anxiety has not gone away, but has increased and comes up regularly, and is difficult to deal with.

‘I see US Marines landing, holding their rifles above water; the long stretch of sand, the sandy beaches, frenzied activity, thousands disembarking. The sea is calm, the water still, gentle ripples breaking against the shore. There is no personal thought or fear, but mammoth coordination, working as one mind, one armoured body, almost a feeling of buoyancy, testosterones flying high.

I hear the seagulls crying in the distance. I see long blades of grass rising on the edge of the deserted beach against a pale sky. I do not know where this is. I am not there. I do not see myself in it. I take a long breath. I feel the warmth, the softness of the sand caving in under my feet, but do not see myself, though I am there somehow.

A German Soldier suddenly appears out of nowhere. He looks lost. Where is he?' I am sitting in my chair as I write this, and I am that German Soldier, in uniform and helmet. It is confusing. I take a long breath. I start crying.

Berlin

'I am a tall, blond, teenage Soldier, one of Hitler's Children Army fighting in Berlin. I have no experience of fighting, my training was short, and I am not prepared for what I see. I am crying as I write this. All is rubble and death around me. Berlin is destroyed, bodies all over, emerging from under collapsed buildings which stand like skeletons against the sky. A terrible sight, rubble and dust, an Apocalyptic view of what was once a thriving city. This memory of Berlin haunts me. I cry.

I was born in Nazi Germany and had no other experience of life. I was part of Hitler's Youth. I was selected, my parents had no choice. They simply took me away to train me. I was selected for my good, 'German' looks: tall, blond. When the Reich was falling apart, we were thrown into the mire, Hitler's last resort, an Army made of children and old people. What an inglorious end! The Futility of it all!' I was confused.

I ask myself: What happens next? as there is a Pause, a Silence, an Emptiness. I am still in uniform, helmet and boots, as I write this, but am beginning to be weary.

'Where is my Family? I see nothing but Destruction and Death, people scavenging for food amidst the ruins, like hungry dogs. Where am I?

A sudden vision of blades of grass against the sky and a

long, deserted beach. Images of another Life, Soldiers with distinctive uniforms and berets, horses, from end 19th Century Germany [?]'

It is confusing. I feel tired and stressed and I stop. Will resume tomorrow hoping to discover more about this teenage German Soldier. What happened to him? [27.2.19]

The End of The War-Berlin [1945]

197.Surrender

Last night I felt the onset of two panic attacks. Very scary. Fortunately, I managed to stop them. There is a Past Life which is trying to surface and it must be an important one, judging by the energy attached to it. I will try now and see what happens.

'While I was relaxing in preparation for the regression, the year '1945' came to me and I saw the actual numbers written, so to speak, very clearly: '1945', the year when the War ended. I enter a Dark Tunnel and start the Journey. It is pitch dark, but I walk through it. I see Berlin, a picture of Desolation and Death: crumbling buildings, rubble, dust, chaos, confusion, Allied Soldiers, German Soldiers, what a mess! Where am I in all this?

I am a German Soldier in uniform, boots, and helmet. I am sitting in my chair as I write this. I do not see his face well, shadowed by the helmet. I go down the Well of Darkness and bring up the Darkness that torments my Soul. I dive into it. Slimy, unpleasant, unyielding-like swimming in a sea of mud. I see a very confusing picture: top German military, Russian Soldiers. I keep seeing a German General, very vividly. I do not know who he is. I see Germany surrender, signing of papers.

Where am I in all this?' [28.2.19]

198.Berlin 1944

'I again start a regression. After a while, '1945' appears clearly in my mind's eye. Again, I see images of a devastated, totally destroyed Berlin, buried in rubble and dust, skeleton buildings standing like broken teeth. What a sight!' I am beginning to feel pain in my solar plexus and I dive into it, into its dark, murky waters. It is like a deep, dark abyss and I do not know what I will find as I dig deeper and deeper into the unconscious. As I go deeper into the pain, I feel the resistance give way. I take a deep breath.

'Actually, the year 1944[110] appears in black and white, Soldiers fighting in the background. I see German Soldiers. I start rolling to and fro on my chair, as I penetrate the dark mass of unconscious memories. Images of Hitler, when the going was good, again a Nazi Soldier but I do not see his face. It is confusing. 1944, appears again.' I am astonished. I do not see myself, but suddenly, I am sitting in my chair as I write in full German uniform, complete with helmet and boots.

'I see military marches, banners, so impressive, so misleading. I see Generals, including Rommel, images of a recent Past. What have I got to do with all this? Who am I? Why am I here?

I see a young Nazi Officer [possibly late 20s/early 30s] very blond, with wavy hair, very good-looking. Who is He? He has some decorations on his collar and I am him and now write this. Weird. [5.3.19]

HMS Sikh [Tunisia-13 December 1941]

There is an interference from another Life as a First Lieutenant of HMS Sikh in the Battle of Cape Bon, Tunisia, when I died the Night of December 13th, 1941. [Same Soul]. My name was D.E. Cole-Hamilton. The following may also be an interference from another Life.

'I see bombs falling on the sea, exploding with great splashes of water and light into the air. The submarine is torpedoed. I see the despair on the Commander's young and beautiful Face. The submarine has come up, but bombs fall thick and fast - there is no salvation. Some of the crew have jumped into the icy waters, others are trapped inside. I see the water flooding the belly of the boat with great force, hitting the men inside it. What a way to die!

I go deeper and deeper, and rock to and fro in my chair in

great agitation as I witness the very last moments of those brave Men. The noise, the screaming, the gushing water - what a terrible sight!

It is quickly over. The boat is sinking fast. Where am I? I am 25 years old, in the full beauty and promise of my young Life. I cry. I have a young wife and a small child. I cry.' I do not see where I am.' I will stop shortly because I feel tired. 'The boat is reaching the sea-bed - all inside are dead, including myself.'
I will investigate tomorrow. He was with me for a long time afterwards, observing me in this new Life. I feel so very sorry for him, for what he missed out of his life then. [5.3.19]

199.1944-A Russian and German Soldier-Berlin

I am still experiencing moments of great fear, anxiety, and even the onset of panic attacks-which fortunately have not materialised, the intensity of which I have never experienced before and is very terrifying. I thought I could die if I had a fully blown one. They happen always at night, sometimes during the day, but they are not so fierce, I wonder why. There is more to discover and I try a regression.

'As I sink into the Unconscious, I begin to see faint images of a broken City, all dust and rubble against a livid sky. I see a young Russian Soldier very faintly, but not his face. I feel pain in my stomach which increases in intensity as I continue.

There is resistance. '1944' again comes to mind. I go dep into the pain and do not know what the pain is, just feel it in my solar plexus. Suddenly, I feel very hot. I am a German Soldier sitting in my chair, writing this, in uniform, helmet and boots. I take a deep breath and ask myself: Who are you? It is confusing. Also, a snapshot from Normandy, all at once.

A promontory with long blades of grass sloping down to a long stretch of sandy beach, [Juno Beach], US Marines disembarking. I am beginning to feel tired and ask myself:

Who am I? How old am I?

The Russians are Coming

Nineteen. I am nineteen years old and fighting a war I do not understand. My training was short and I am not prepared for what I see. I am scared. We are a small group of young recruits. With others, we hold parts of Berlin, but the Russians are approaching with mad fury. The fighting intensifies. We hold our positions, but for how long? What will happen to us?

I think about my Parents-where are they?

They must have left before the Russians came so close. I hope so. We are hiding inside a building, snipers, ready to shoot. The Russians are approaching, we hold our positions, but are running out of ammunitions.

THEY FIND US!'

I feel tired and stop. I do not want to know, or see, what happened, just now. I will go back tomorrow. [9.3.19]

202.A German Soldier

My anxiety attacks have increased in frequency and intensity, they keep me awake at night, so much that I hate going to bed. I decided to try a Regression again, but it may not be easy with a deep-seated trauma. I need to resolve this issue. There is a great weight, oppression, on my heart chakra.

'I am in a dark Tunnel, but there is an opening and some Light in the distance. As I go slowly back in Time, my face is changing, the air is rarefied. I wear a helmet, uniform, boots. I am a German Soldier.' I feel a wave of intense pain rising from my solar plexus engulfing me. I dig deeper and deeper into the unconscious to bring up memories, no matter how terrifying they might me. Who are you- I ask - What is your name?

There is a lot of interference: American Soldiers disembarking in Normandy, Nazi Generals, Himmler, Soviet Soldiers, it is very chaotic. They all drop in and interrupt me constantly. I try to shut them out, but it is difficult. I have been over one hour into the regression and it is getting more and more chaotic and confusing - just as it truly was back in 1945, when the War reached its final spasm. [30.3.19]

203.A German Soldier

I am trying again to go back to that Life which is now causing me uninterrupted anxiety and fear of everything, but the resistance is very great, as there must be a great trauma.

'I see the German Soldier, but not his face. I see him by profile and now he has turned his back on me. I am that German Soldier. I am seized by a fit of convulsion and coughing fit that leaves me exhausted and out of breath, tears running down my cheeks, so intense it was.

The Face is partly obscured by the helmet. I see a Battlefield, Hell broken loose, intense fighting going on against a livid sky and burnt-out trees, like skeletons.

I feel very hot. I am all in a sweat. Intense fear. I breathe it in the air, it is all pervasive. The air is thick with smoke. I can hardly breathe. I can hardly see in front of me. Suddenly, a young Soldier in uniform and boots, no helmet, but a 'triangular' cap, appears. I see his face clearly. A small face, rather a pointed face. I recognise him. He reminds me of that World War II Aviator, and of the First Lieutenant of HMS Sikh. It is the same Soul in different Incarnations and they look very much the same. I do not know if he is German, perhaps a Cadet. I see him marching, with others. He is definitely German. He is sitting in my chair, uniform, helmet, and boots. Who are you? I ask-What is your name? I see a young, pale and anguished Face.'

An Execution

I take a deep breath and plunge into the dark, muddy mass of the unconscious Past, deep into my Solar Plexus. I begin to feel ill as I do so, going deeper and deeper into it, rocking to and fro in my chair, in an effort to access details, but it is very difficult. I am feeling tired andwant to end the session, but continue. I feel horribly hot and I am wet with perspiration. Very, very unpleasant.

'I see a Firing Squad.' [31.3.19]

A Pilgrimage to Normandy

Last week I visited Normandy, all the Battlefields of the

Invasion which signalled the beginning of the end of the War. I visited all the Beaches, Omaha, Utah, Juno, Gold, Sword. I was overwhelmed by a mixture of feelings as an American Marine and as a German Soldier, as memories were stirred up. I was struck by the beauty of Juno Beach in particular. I recognised the Dunes, the long blades of grass, as I walked up the promontory retracing my steps as that German Soldier. I felt how privileged I was to be able to glide through Past and Present and revisit places where I had been before. A weird feeling to be again on a Beach where I had been over 70 years earlier. [24.10.19]

Japan

45.Kamikaze -A Youth Denied

'The Kamikaze[22] was a very young and beautiful young man in his very early twenties, with a very sweet face, romantic, very much in love with a young woman. He was very shy and never had the courage to tell her and she married someone else. He did not declare his love because he lacked confidence in himself. Although he loved her deeply, he had not even thought of the responsibility of marriage and a family of his own. He was not mature enough for her to even see him as an attractive man. He needed someone to explore life with, whereas she needed someone to guide her. He needed a peer she needed a father figure. Although close friendship between them, attraction as lovers was not in her awareness.

She never knew the depth of his feelings for her. She was traditional and would have followed her parents' wishes. He only joked with her about his love, he never really made her understand the extent of the emotion. He did not offer her the future she was hoping for. He should have declared his love in the traditional manner and she would have listened. She still did not love him and really needed an older man to help her form her character and to make decisions for her.

His parents did not want him to take this post, but he was fired by enthusiasm and never mentioned his failed love again.

Sadness and disappointment filled him before he chose this end. There was no point in his life. He gave his devotion to his country instead of his love to another human being. He died soon afterwards on a mission. She had a long life and she was still alive in the mid-90s.'

I am overcome by extreme sadness.

Battle Of Midway [1942][127]

172.Battle on a Pacific Island

I have been feeling extremely sad in the past few days, so I decided to do a regression. As I start, there is tension, sadness, a feeling of oppression in my heart chakra. Tears in my heart. I feel slightly sick. Overwhelming sadness. I do not know what is the cause of this sadness. It fills my chest. Feel the pain and let go. It is a deep sorrow which has no voice, cannot express itself except by the intensity of its pain. Raw, unpolished sorrow. I take a few, deep, breaths. 'The caducity of Life'. This blind pain is right up in the chest, under the neck and shoulder blades. I still do not know what it is all about.

'I see Japanese Soldiers with bayonets in a forest. I see their faces very clearly, wearing small berets [caps] on their heads. Is it an island? I see trees and foliage. I am a Japanese Soldier and am sitting in my chair, writing this. I see Emperor Hirohito[126] wearing a dark suit. I see the island again, planes in the sky, some are shot down in a fireball. The sound of explosion, the smell of burnt metal, crushing on land and sea, with big splashing noise. Do I know who I am? I ask myself. What is my name?

I look impenetrable, my face is made of stone, my eyes staring ahead of me, lost in thoughts. How old am I? I do not look more than 35/36. I do not know what I am doing on this island. There is a battle going on. I do not expect to survive this, we are fighting to the Death, desperately holding our positions.

I feel pain in my chest. Complex feelings and confusion cross my mind. My family comes from a very long line of

Samurai warriors. Like all Japanese Soldiers, my commitment to the Emperor is total, boundless…and yet, the snakehead of Doubt rises in my heart.

A Brutal Death

The War is brutal, fierce and bloody. We are not afraid of Death. We welcome Death. A Death on the battlefield is honourable and to be wished for. What will the outcome of this be? I move forward cautiously, I do not see my Soldiers, dense undergrowth. My heart is pounding, full of unbearable pain. Suddenly, I step on a grenade/explosive and I am blown up to pieces! What was my name?

My name was Hiroshi Mitzuki.

I leave a wife and two children.' [28.8.17]

207.Marines

In the last weeks, I have had the beginning of panic attacks at night [always at night], including last night, really bad, difficult to breathe. I need to regress to a Past Life. As soon as I start my Mother is with me.

'I see on my left-hand side, this Marine, helmet, rifle, the lot. Is he wearing a sort of net around his helmet?' Feel pain in my chest. 'I see the dirty face of this young Marine, crying in pain?' I see these images in black and white, not in colour as sometimes I do. Where is he? I descend into my solar plexus to dig up the Past. I see other Marines lying flat on some raised point in the ground, their rifles ready to fire, they too are wearing short nets around their helmet, some with leaves stuck in them. Where are we?

As I deep dive into my solar plexus and into the Past, a Shadow rises in front of me [going through death to access the Past]. I ask the Shadow to let me pass into the Realm of the Dead. I still see this Marines, there are trees, where are we? 'Battle of Midway' comes through. I need more information.

'I see Marines on the assault - I am beneath them, under their feet, as they spring on the attack. I am slowly turning into this Marine, my body is changing, what a transformation! I am in Uniform, a rucksack on my back, boots, helmet with net and a few leaves, surrounded by trees [a jungle?] I move forward with caution. Where am I? - I ask again. 'Battle of Midway' comes through. I am this Marine, sitting in my chair, my head reclined on my heart. Who are you? I ask myself. Show your face to me. I see more Marines landing on a beach - it is an island.

Japanese Soldiers

I now see Japanese Soldiers, their berets/caps. I see them clearly, particularly this Officer. He addresses his Soldiers [half naked] in a clearing in a forest. What is going on? I am that Japanese Officer, now sitting in my chair, I see his face very clearly, lost in thoughts, impenetrable. I wear trousers tucked in knee-high leather boots, jacket with waist belt, another across my chest. I have authority, who am I? 'Battle of Midway' comes through again. I see this Japanese Camp where men are relaxing. It is hot and humid, unpleasant. I see this man, half naked, no uniform, no weapons, is he a peasant Soldier? He is moving in the thick undergrowth. He is not old, possibly mid-thirties, with very short hair. I catch a glimpse of the Island in the sunshine, the sea is calm.

I am now the Marine again, with the rucksack on my back, ankle boots, helmet with short net covering most of my face. I am young. I move to and fro in my chair, restless, in growing agitation. I feel hot. 'What am I doing here?' I ask myself. Something BIG is moving in my chest, rising from the solar plexus. I am good-looking, blond hair from under my helmet. I am distressed. I feel pain in my chest. Something difficult to release.

I am now the Japanese Officer and he, too, looks distressed, lost in thoughts. I feel pain in my heart. Other Lives intrude on me and I send them away. There is a large square in an ancient town, I see Emperor Hirohito. What is my name? There is a very beautiful Japanese woman in a kimono and I am her, sitting in my chair. Do not know who she is. I also see an image of an earlier warrior, a Samurai.

I go back to the Japanese Officer. Tell me who you are and what happened to you? - I ask - hurry up, I am tired. What is your name? 'Toshiro Mifune [?]' he answers. What happened to you?

I am increasingly tired and want to close. I see Marines moving on in the Island. I feel pain in my chest and I am agitated, want to close, but cannot do so. I go back to the Marine, there is a big trauma, difficult to release. I see a big plane with coffins covered with the Flag with the Stars belching out of its metal tummy. What happened, how did you die, what was your name? I ask in great agitation, cannot sit still in my chair. I am going to close soon.

I see the Japanese Officer and the Shadow of Death behind him. I urge him to speak. I sink into the solar plexus in an effort to speed things up and close. It is dark and murky as I sink deeper and deeper.

What happened to the Marine? I cannot dig up things from the depths of the unconscious. There is too much resistance. I see him clearly. He is lying on the ground and has taken his helmet off, revealing hair cropped short with blond curls, very good-looking, early twenties.' Complex lives, will go back tomorrow. [1.6.21]

Marine - Japanese Officer

I have felt great oppression in my heart chakra and know must try to access these two Past Lives, before they cause panic attacks. As I listen to my music, it begins to cut through hidden emotions, works its magic and slowly takes me back. 'I see a Marine landing on a beach.' Something stirs in my stomach and I feel a burning pain. 'I see him on a beach, long blades of grass, is it Normandy? Is he alone? Pain in my stomach. 'He is now sitting in my chair, helmet, muddy boots, rucksack.' Pain in my upper chest. Oppressive. Difficult to access.

'I now see this Japanese Officer in a forest. cap, Khaki shirt with pockets, what is he doing? He has noweapons, is in a jungle clearing. I have a very heavy chest, do not see other Soldiers, strange. I feel great pain in my chest and agitation. Where are the Soldiers? Tension in my throat. Something is trying to come up, but it is extremely difficult. I am close to the truth and yet distant, it eludes me. The pain is under the collar bone, under the throat, but cannot release it. One last attempt. I see a vast mass of calm water [the Pacific], a lone sandy beach, tropical trees. I focus on this Japanese Officer, my head sunk on my chest, but am tired and close the session. [6.6.21]

An Illusion of Peace

I decided to try to go back to these Past Lives, because they are bothering me and the anxiety is growing, it is not going away.

'It is the same Japanese Officer I saw 2 days ago, cap, khaki shirt with pockets, strange, I see trees behind him, tropical, the calm, azure sea [Pacific]. It is so calm, as if there was no war going on. I am this Man, sitting in my chair and writing this. There is a clearing in the jungle, Japanese Soldiers sitting on the ground half naked. I am talking to them.

Suddenly, another vision: Marines, small nets around their helmets, planes in the sky, pain in my solar plexus. Marines landing on the Island. It looks deserted. I start rocking in my chair, my head down on my chest. I stare at the calm sea. My home too, is an island. I come from a long line of Samurais…Duty to the Emperor is paramount in my life. What will happen next? My commitment is total, unbreakable - and yet, the snakehead of doubt creeps in. I am troubled by this. Am I questioning my loyalty to the Emperor?

The Marines are in the jungle - no enemy in sight. Is there a War going on? It is very hot, clothes sticking to the skin, heavy perspiration, uncomfortable. 'Battle of Midway' comes through again. I feel oppressed in my heart. I am now this Marine, sitting in my chair. I am young. Do I want to be in this War? No, I do not want to be here.

I am tired I want to close. The Martine is still here, I have pain in my heart. I see explosions, it is bits and pieces and I close, the Marine and Japanese Officer are still here, though, do not want to leave. I close on them. Till next time. [8.6.21]

Westerbork Transit Camp[107] Drenthe Province North-Eastern Netherlands

181.A Pilgrimage to a Nazi Past

I fulfilled a long-standing wish and went to Krakow, Auschwitz - Birkenau, Bergen-Belsen, Theresienstadt, among others. An emotional rollercoaster.

Westerbork

We visited Westerbork[107] in north-eastern Holland, where Jews, including Anne Frank and her Family[108], were deported. No-one died there, as the newly arrived were promptly transported to various Concentration Camps and put to the Gas Chambers. The Camp is now empty, the wooden structures [barracks] having decayed long ago, but barbed wire and turrets enclosing the Camp are still there. I walked the whole length and breadth of the Camp, now filled with vegetation and trees, but strangely, no birds, no sound, no chirrups, no animals, no life in the Camp and the forest around it. All dead. Eerie. I was overwhelmed by the size of the Camp and this vast Emptiness filled with meaning. As I approached the end of the Camp, ready to leave, I turned my head and looked back.

'A crowd of women, men, young and old, children, well-dressed, with suitcases, [recent arrivals back then] stood only a few yards from me. A beautiful young woman, right in the front, perhaps in her late twenties- early thirties, a brunette with wavy, shoulder-length hair, dark eyes and red mouth, wearing a grey coat, looked at me straight into the eye as if to challenge me. I held that gaze for some time, and then turned my head and walked away with a heavy heart. They did not try to follow me as I silently blessed them in my heart and said 'Goodbye'. I later saw those suitcases at Auschwitz, in a dimly-lit glass enclosure, the leather having become translucent in its last stages of exudation, dissipation, and decay, the suitcases having survived their tragic owners for over seventy years and being their last

Reliquaries. I wondered how much longer they would last. I cannot stop crying as I re-live this experience. [2-13.10.17]

Chapter 20

The Vietnam War

206.A Vietnamese Life [1955]

I DECIDED TO go on a Shamanic Journey to discover blockages which I had not dealt with, and did not expect to see a Past Life as a Vietnamese Soldier in the Vietnam War which lasted twenty years [November 1955 - April 1975]. I saw myself as this young Soldier [early twenties] helmet and rifle moving with difficulty through dense vegetation. I will have to investigate this Life which may be the cause a recent anxiety, agitation and sleeplessness. [26.4.21]

Other Wars

47.A Snapshot

'British commander, wearing jungle - style combat uniform and purple velvet cap [quite recent]'

73.Green Uniforms and Purple Berets

'I tried to connect to Ancient Egypt, but modern-day British Soldiers kept coming in, wearing their green uniforms and velvet purple-violet berets. They were all young and good-looking and smiling [one is here with me as I write this] they all joined together in a group, as if posing for a photograph for me, arms on one another's shoulders, relaxed and smiling'. [3.8.13]

146.Recent Wars

'I see modern Soldiers [Afghanistan?].' [11.1.16]

Chapter 21

More Lives

12.Sole Provider-A Bitter Life

'A LIFE TRAPPED by poverty and the ignorance of those around me having to provide for a large family of brothers and sisters. I wanted a life of prayer and seclusion and was unable to achieve it. I tired and was sad, life was all work and no joy.' I felt the frustration of that Life for days.

13.The Weight of Responsibility

'Many difficult Lives with lots to do and others to look after. Lots of responsibility. In one, my husband is ill and I have to take care of him. It is all very difficult for me, but I somehow manage.' [11.12.96]

20.A Landslide

'I died in an avalanche/landslide. I was pinned down by stones overtaking me as I ran on a mountain side just outside a city in Italy or Greece. I am hopeless and unable to move. Breathing is difficult, enormous pressure on the lungs making it harder and harder to breathe. I am struggling to escape but my strength is not enough. I stay alive through the night and can just see the sky and the moon overhead. I fear dying at night. It reminds me of a dream I had as a child and believe that my soul will be hurt by creatures of the night. I manage to survive till morning when the sun comes into the sky and I see the sunrise colours. I slip into death but feeling safe and protected by the daylight. I am a young girl, only in my teenage years and quite beautiful too. It seems so sad as I think of all the things I will not be able to do before I die.

I accept death, but it was an accident, a mistake. My parents had told me to leave my walk till the next day, but I knew better and went to my death. I left the village to meet a friend from the next village, as I felt I could not disappoint her, only to discover when I got there that she had stayed at home and followed her parents' advice. I also wanted to pick some flowers which got crushed with me in the landslide. [17.3.98]

28.A Glimpse

'I travel through a forest in a covered coach. I am going to be married and some people are with me.' [14.11.98]

29.A Nomadic Life Long Time Ago

'A life wandering through the sandbanks-nomadic people-as a wanderer.

I have a hard life. I am gifted with intuition. I always know where food will be and water, yet I do not believe in my own gifts, but others do. I am in constant doubt and inner conflict as I deny myself in this way.' [9.3.99]

50.A Terrifying Past Life Dream: Egypt

'I was in Egypt, by the sea, staying in a hotel. I walked on the beach by the side of a big mound of sand, like a small mountain or hill, when it began to disintegrate, like an avalanche, creating a huge mass of dust which enveloped everything, including myself and other people. I tried to run away from it and ran into the sea. I could not breathe and I thought 'I am going to die chocking or I am going to drown'. It was very frightening. The cloud of dust was very thick, could not see anything, I felt my way forward, grabbed a leg of a woman who was trying to escape like me and together we managed to return to the safety of the hotel, on the other side of the mound, far away. We went to our rooms, shaken but safe. I spoke to another guest of the terrifying experience and got ready for refreshment. My room's door/window was open and I could see the fallen sand mound and the sea in the distance.' [4.6.13]

55.16th Century Man

'I saw a 16th Century man, possibly a priest, with a black cap like a university graduate, long black tunic, ankle length, and a white sleeveless top on it reaching below the knee like modern priests. He had a short beard and a long, thin moustache reaching the sides of his cheeks near his ears, do not know who he is. I saw soldiers like those painted by Franz Hals[33]'Felt a very deep-seated pain in the solar plexus-a trauma. He was with me for a long time, but could not discover more about his life [27.6.13].

67.Dutch Merchant Girl [16th Century]

'At first, I saw Jesus like He was painted in medieval paintings, round face, eyebrows and eyes, straight, thin nose, short and round black beard and moustache. I then saw a young woman, pretty, not beautiful, small face with high cheekbones, a small hat, travelling frock, at first thought 19th Century, but probably earlier. Saw a harbour, a ship, people boarding the ship, the young woman-first on a carriage holding a small suitcase on her lap, and then the harbour, then other people and lost track of her.

A thought suddenly flashed through my mind: 'The boat went down!'

I saw a large, life-sized portrait of a man dressed in rich black velvet clothes, a bit bald on top, white hair, beard and moustache, with a strong resemblance to the young woman, possibly in his early 50s. Then I saw another large full-size portrait of a lady, possibly in her 50s, with very lively piercing eyes looking directly at you from the painting, also richly dressed in black, unaware of the tragedy that would befell them. They both looked straight out of a painting by Franz Hals[33]. I think they were Dutch merchants, rich household. Saw other men, also as if they had come out from Franz Hals' paintings. They must all have belonged to that period'. I felt an almost unbearable pain in my heart chakra, very strong and overpowering. I found it difficult to let it go, so deep, so powerful it was. It affected me for days. [24.7.13]

70.Visions

Did a Shamanic journey. One-hour long.

'I saw an Indian man, an encampment with tepees at night and some Indians gathered around a fire, then a beautiful Raven, it went up into the night sky, and I saw it again later a few times, very close, in front of me, staring at me. I saw Tutankhamun and Ankhesenamun for a long time, then a wise Old Woman, a Crone, her head and shoulders covered with a long, dark mantle, aquiline nose, very much like the witch [the Queen] in Snow White tale. Then a very clear image of a beautiful full moon, a disk of pure white-silvery light against the dark blue sky and the silhouette of the Old Woman on a broomstick cut against it, flying up the sky.

There was a beautiful little boy, perhaps 5 years old: he looked as if he had just come out of a painting by Rubens: small round face, rosy cheeks and lips, blond curly hair, and a small hat, and later another boy, perhaps 7 or 8 years old, short, blond, wavy hair, with a dark-blue jacket, much later period, perhaps the same boy. Henry VIII appeared briefly, then a Nun with a Crown of Thorns and another Nun-do not know who they are.

I saw the Old Crone again and then a sort of dark rectangular platform with 4 or 5 Grim Reapers at its corners, with fires between them, holding their Sickles, the 'Black Death' flashed through my mind. I was one of them, but not on the platform. I felt I was one of them. I almost certainly died in the Black Death.

A young man appeared, blond curly hair in dark-blue uniform with gold medals, a Prince, holding a helmet under his arm, perhaps the same boy, and then Royalty, William and Kate on their wedding day, and also later in their lives; and more Indians appeared.' [30.7.13]

83.A Dutch Maid-17th Century

'Then a Dutch-looking young maid appeared, dressed like the maids in Vermeer's paintings, long gown, camisole, with a triangular scarf on her shoulders and another one tied around her head'.

200.The Wailing Wall-Jerusalem

'I was in the middle of a meditation when suddenly I saw this man, a Jew, with small round hat in the middle of the head, short hair, thick beard, longer in the front [about 3-4 cm] and shorter at the sides [1-2 cm] with a round, chubby face, gold-rimmed spectacles, staring at me. I then saw the Wailing Wall in Jerusalem and this man [maybe thirty-five years old] wearing a long, black hat and two curls-one on each side of his face, and a long, black coat, among the many people praying there.'

I laid down to rest, he became me and laid down on the bed fully dressed, hat and all. It was an extremely clear and powerful vision which caught me by surprise. [9.3.19]

Visitors

61.Various

'My two Sikh Guides [turban, moustache and beard], one young one old, appeared and also a Bishop, but I do not think he was a Pope, in full ceremonial clothes, wearing glasses. Then I saw a young Friar, with blond hair, good looking, also in ceremonial clothes-do not know who they are. And then, again, another Bishop [?] and another Friar came to me.' [22.7.13]

71.Dropping In-Many Popes

Then something extraordinary happened: out of the blue came Pope Roncalli-John XXII; Pope Francis I, and Pope John Paul II[44]. I saw them for a considerable time, especially Pope Francis

I and caught a glimpse of Pope Pius XII [Pope Pacelli[45]] the controversial Pope of World War II. They were all dressed in pure white'. [31.7.13]

82.Black Cat

Tonight, I had an extraordinary experience. I fed the little black cat which had visited me so very regularly and held him in my arms, close to my heart, like a baby, and I bent down to kiss him on his little head. As I did so, I felt a great wave of love for this wonderful little being. I suddenly ceased to exist in my present earthly form, I had no feelings or thoughts, as my

physical body disappeared and was superimposed by a transparent vapour-like shaft slightly denser at the bottom, where there were strands [lines] of pale colours like hues of blue, pink, mauve, and much lighter going toward the top, where it was pale white and where there was the very faint outline of a head, bent down towards the cat, which this extraordinary presence held in his arms, which also were only faintly outlined. I felt it was a male presence, though I was not there-he replaced me. This presence was very tall, possibly three metres high and looked down at the cat with love, which saw him and lifted his head with a start, but was not frightened. Then the cat wanted to stay with me but I had to leave him outside. [23.8.13]

89.A Strange Occurrence

I opened the front door at about 2 am at night and saw a tall, slim, man fast approaching, only a few metres away, he was marching and stomping his feet on the pavement with great noise-tomp, tomp, tomp. I waited for him to pass me by and saw his face briefly in the streetlight, but no features, still too far. He quickly came my way, a tall grey shadow wearing a dark grey coat and turned his head and looked straight at me [I was in full light] as he walked away very quickly, but I could not see his face, his face was concealed by a shadow as was his body. Only later I realized what a very strange experience that had been. [18.9.13]

169.Diana Princess of Wales [1961-1997]

Princess Diana suddenly appears-she came to me earlier on. She is wearing a pale-green suit and she is in her 30s. Suddenly I disappear and she sits in my chair. Mother Theresa is also here and stands behind me as I write this. They both visited me last week and were with me for a long time. Mother Theresa's face is close to mine, old and lined like the trunk of an old tree.

A Cosmic Vision

Wilfred is here, too. I see multiple things at once: Diana, Wilfred, the Canal, the Battlefields, all rolled up into one vision. I do not know what to make of this. Mother Theresa is opposite me, very close. She looks troubled as if she wants to say something. It is weird. The Roman General of my Past Incarnations also appears in glorious uniform, steel helmet and red-rust mantle. All rolled up into One. This Sphere I see is like the Earth, but rather than Continents I see people. I am confused, I do not know the meaning of this.

A Message for William and Harry

Diana is here again. I see her smiling in her green suit. I see her younger, shy, her head bowed down, so very much like William's. Are you happy about the boys? I ask her. 'Yes, they turned out well and I am proud of them. I am never far away. I love them dearly as always and follow in their footsteps, trying to protect them.'

What would you advise them? I ask softly.

'Follow your heart and do what you think is right. Love your family as much as I love you. Know that you are not alone, for I am with you always.' [21.8.17]

Notes

All references are from Wikipedia, unless otherwise stated.

[1]**Before the hostilities**, marriage between colonists and Indians were not so unusual.

[2]**Rounded crown with uraeus, the Khepresh**, the Blue Crown or War Crown of the New Kingdom Pharaohs in battle and in ceremonies. The uraeus was a symbol ofthe Goddess Wadjet, one of the earliest Egyptian deities, often depicted as a cobra, the serpent goddess. She became the patroness of the Nile Delta and the protector of all Lower Egypt.

[3]**Pope Innocent** [1161-1216] was one of the most powerful and influential popes. At the time of his accession to the papacy, he was only thirty-seven years of age.

[4]**Pope Boniface VIII** [1235-1303] claimed spiritual and temporal power over European kings and was especially challenged by Philip IV of France and by the Poet Dante Alighieri, who placed him in the Eight Circle of Hell in his Divine Comedy, among the Simoniacs.

[5]The **Taurus Mountains** are a mountain range in Anatolia [Southern Turkey].

[6]**Susa** was an ancient feudal state in Italy, and also one of the most important cities of the Ancient Near East [in Ancient Southern Iran] capital of Elam and the Achaemenid Empire.

[7]**Seti I** [d. 1279 BC]- New Kingdom, 19th Dynasty, son of Ramesses I [1293-1291BC] a 'career' army officer who

succeeded Horemheb, the last Pharaoh of the 18th Dynasty, and father of Ramesses II the Great [1279-1212 BC] perhaps the Pharaoh of the Biblical story of the Exodus.

[8]**Bronislaw Bohatyrewicz** [1870-1940] was a Polish Commander and a General of the Polish Army. He was arrested by the NKVD and imprisoned at Kozelsk [Polish for Katyn] Concentration Camp in the Soviet Union. He was murdered in Katyn Massacre in the spring of 1940 aged seventy. He was one of the Generals whose bodies were identified by forensic scientists of the Katyn Commission during the 1943 exhumation.

Colonel Pawlikowski was Commander of the Fighter Brigade who began the September campaign to defend Warsaw after the German's attack on Poland. He was killed in 1943 while leading a Polish fighter wing over the English Channel. [Why Air Forces Fail: The Anatomy of Defeat]

[9] **Johannes Erwin Eugen Rommel** [1891- 1944], known as the Desert Fox, was Field Marshal in the Wehrmacht of Nazi Germany during WWII. He was forced by Hitler to commit suicide.

[10] **Ramesses II,** Ramesses the Great, [ca1303-1213 BC] was the 3rd Pharaoh of the 19th Dynasty of Egypt.

[11]**Anne Boleyn** [ca. 1501-1536] was Queen of England from 1533 to 1536, the second wife of Henry VIII and Marquess of Pembroke in her own right. Anne married **Henry VIII** in 1533. Their marriage marked the beginning of the split between Rome and the Church of England.

[12]**Catherine Parr,** [1512-1548] Queen of England and Ireland [1543-47] was the sixth and last wife of Henry VIII [1491-1547]. Six months after his death, she married his brother-in-law, Thomas Seymour, but died shortly after giving birth to a daughter, Mary Seymour who was very short-lived. She had four husbands.

[13]**Henry VIII** [1491-1547] was the second Tudor monarch, son of Henry VII.

[14]**Elizabeth I** [1533-1603] daughter of Henry VIII and Anne Boleyn, was the last monarch of the Tudor Dynasty.

[15]**Thomas Seymour** [1508-1549-] 1st Baron Seymour of Sudeley, was the brother of the English Queen Jane Seymour [1508-1537] the third wife of Henry VIII and mother of **Edward VI** [1537-1553] He was the fourth husband of Catherine Parr. Thomas Seymour was executed less than a year after Catherine's death for treason against Edward VI, Henry's only child. In less than three years Catherine, Thomas and little Mary were all dead.

[16]**Wounded Knee**, on the Lakota Pine Ridge Indian Reservation in South Dakota, USA, is where two wars between North American Indians and representatives of the US Government were fought, which in 1890 ended in the massacre of around 300 Sioux - mostly old men, women and children. They were shovelled into a long and narrow mass grave which bears the same name.

[17]**Tutankhamun,** the last legitimate Pharaoh of the 18th Dynasty in Egypt [r. ca 1347-1337 BC]. After Carter's discovery of his tomb in 1922, he became the most famous of all Egyptian pharaohs and a symbol of Egypt. [Ancient Egypt: A Social History, p184]

Smenkhare [1351-1348 BC] ruled between Akhenaten and Tutankhamun. [Ancient Egypt: A Social History, Cambridge University Press, p.184]

[18]**Claudius I** [1 August 1, 10 BC-October 13, 54 AD]was born in Gaul [France] into the Roman Imperial family. **Tiberius,** the second emperor of Rome, was his uncle. He was an efficient administrator and builder of many new roads, aqueducts, and canals across the Empire. In 43 AD Claudius undertook the conquest of Britain. He conquered Mauretania [North Africa], Thrace [the Balkans] and Lycia [part of Turkey]. He married

twice, first with Messalina and had two children from her, Britannicus and Octavia. After she was executed for plotting against him with a consul, he married his niece Agrippina the Younger, who with her son Domitius [Nero] was the only surviving direct descendant of Augustus. He was poisoned, probably by his wife, and died on 13 October 54 AD. **Nero** became Emperor.

[19]**Toga,** a garment of Ancient Rome, a long cloth [12 to 20 feet in length] draped over shoulders and around the body, worn over a tunic.

[20]**31 BC-**A third civil war broke out in Rome following the fight for supremacy between Octavian and Anthony which resulted in the Battle of Actium, on the western coast of Greece, where Anthony's fleet was defeated in 31 BC. He was saved with his remaining forces by the intervention of Cleopatra's fleet which was waiting close by. They were pursued and defeated in Alexandria by Octavian on 1 August 30 BC. Anthony killed himself, as did Cleopatra.

[21]**Samurai** - the military nobility in medieval and early- modern Japan.

[22]**Kamikaze** ['divine wind'] were suicide attacks by pilots from the Empire of Japan against Allied naval vessels in the closing part of the Pacific Campaign of WWII from 1944. Kamikaze pilots were aged between 16 and 24 years.

[23]**Valley of the Kings** where Egypt's pharaohs were buried in tombs dug out of rock after 1500 BC, when pyramid-building came to an end.

Asipia, Eldest Daughter of Amenhotep II [1402-1364 BC*] 7th pharaoh of the 18th Dynasty of Egypt, the First Dynasty of the New Kingdom when Egypt was at the peak of its power, its 'Golden Age', from 1549-1550 BC to 1292 BC. This Dynasty is also known as Thutmosid Dynasty, because of four pharaohs named Thutmose. Many of Egypt's most famous pharaohs were from the 18th Dynasty, including Tutankhamun, Hatshepsut, Akhenaten. [*Ancient Egypt: A Social History, Cambridge University Press, p.184]

[24] **Horus, Her, Heru, Har,** one of the most important ancient Egyptian deities with many functions, most importantly God of kingship and the sky.

[25]**A Tomb in the Desert**, Tutankhamun's tomb in the Valley of the Kings, near Thebes [Luxor].

[26]**The Katyn Forest Massacre** [April-May 1940]. A series of executions, estimated at about 22,000, of Polish Officers and Intelligentsia by the NKVD [Soviet Secret Police] in several locations, but the Massacre took the name from Katyn, Kozelsk, near Smolensk, where Russian concentration camps held 15,000 Polish POWs from October 1939 to February 1940, and where their Mass Graves were first discovered by the invading Nazis in 1942. They broadcasted their discovery to the world in April 1943 to damage the newly formed Alliance between Poland, Western Allies, and the Soviet Union. The Nazis brought in a European Red Cross Committee called the Katyn Commission to exhume and examine the bodies and prove that the Soviets were responsible for the murders, who in turn accused the Nazis. The killings of Katyn by the NKVD included, amongst others, 14 Polish generals of whom Bronislaw Bohatyrewicz [ret.] subsequently mentioned.

[27]**Warsaw**, the capital and largest city of Poland, on the Vistula River.

[28]**Ostashkov.** Another Russian concentration camp for Polish POWs from October 1939 to February 1940.

[29]**Julius Caesar** [July 100- March 15, 44 BC] the greatest and most legendary of Rome's politicians/commanders who became consul of the Roman Republic and dictator for life amid great opposition [which led to his murder] by republican senators. He greatly extended the Roman Empire before seizing power and

making himself dictator of Rome, paving the way for the imperial system.

Roman General. Was contemporary of Julius Caesar, of Marc Anthony [83-30 BC], at the time of the Civil War [31 BC], of Octavian [63 BC-14 AD]. When Caesar was murdered, he was about 37 years old, about 46 when Marc Anthony died, about 59 when Octavian acceded the throne.

[30]**Nicholas II** was born in 1868 and was the last Emperor of Russia, ruling from November 1894 until his forced abdication in March 1917 by the Soviets.

[31]**Tsarina - Princess Alix of Hesse and by Rhine**, wife of Tsar Nicholas II.

[32]The **Children** of the Russian Imperial Family, Grand Duchesses Maria, Olga, Tatiana, Anastasia, Tsarevich Alexei.

[33]**Franz Hals** - A Dutch painter [15th Century]

[34]The town of **El Alamein** is located in the Northern Matrouh Governorate of Egypt on the Mediterranean Sea and the seat of two important Battles of WWII, in July and November 1942, of Military Cemeteries, Germany, Italy, Greece, Commonwealth of Nations.

[35]**Commonwealth Cemetery, El Alamein.**

[36]**Thomas Seymour**, last husband of Queen Catherine Parr.

[37]**Apollo,** in Greek Mythology, was the son of **Zeus** and one of the most important of the Olympian deities. He is god of music, poetry, art, oracles, medicine, sun, light, knowledge, among other things. In ancient Greek sculpture, he was represented as a very beautiful man.

[38]**Nefertiti** [ca.1370-ca.1330 BC] was an Egyptian queen and the Great Royal Wife of Akhenaten, a Pharaoh of the 18th Dynasty, and mother of Ankhesenamun, half-sister and wife of Tutankhamun.

[39]**Gracchi Brothers**, Tiberius and Gaius, were Romans born to a plebeian branch of the old and noble Sempronia family. They served as tribunes in the late 2nd century BC and attempted to pass legislation to redistribute major aristocratic landholdings among the urban poor and veterans. After some initial success, they were assassinated by their enemies.

[40]**Khufu** reigned for 26 years, ca. 2570 BC, a pharaoh of the 4th Dynasty in Egypt, great builders of pyramids.

[41]**Temple of Vesta** in the Roman Forum, where a sacred fire, apparently representing the fortunes of Rome, was permanently kept by the Vestal priestesses. It was round in shape and its entrance faced east, to represent the connection between the fire and the sun as a source of life.

[42]**Erasmus da Rotterdam** [October 1466-July 1536] was a Dutch Renaissance humanist, and Catholic priest, who although he criticized the abuses of the Roman Catholic Church and called for reforms, recognized the authority of the pope.

[43]**Thomas Cranmer** [2 July 1489-21 March 1556] was Archbishop of Canterbury during the reign of Henry VIII and a leader of the English Reformation.

[44]**Pope Saint John XXIII** [Angelo Giuseppe Roncalli] the 'Good Pope' [1881-1963] was Pope from October 1958 to his death. **Pope Francis I** [Jorge Mario Bergoglio] [December 1936] was elected in March 2013. **Pope Saint John Paul II** [Karol Josef Wojtyla] [May 1920-April 2005] was pope from 1978 to his death.

[45]**Pope Pius XII** [Eugenio Maria Giuseppe Giovanni Pacelli] [March 1876-October 1958] was Pope from March 1939 to his death.

[46]**Sekhmet,** was a warrior goddess who protected the Pharaohs in war, and also goddess of healing, depicted as a woman with a lioness head, her cult was dominant in Ancient Egypt.

[47] **Octavian,** later Augustus, [63 BC-August 14 AD] the founder of the Roman Empire and its first Emperor, ruling from 27 BC to his death in AD 14.

[48]**Marc Anthony** [83-30 BC] was a Roman politician and general, an ally of Julius Caesar, and a ruler of Rome's eastern provinces, including Egypt. He married Octavian's sister Octavia, but was the lover of Cleopatra, Queen of Egypt, who bore him three children. He was the main rival of Caesar's successor. The rivalry with Octavian led to Civil War in 31 BC when, at his instigation, the Roman Senate declared war on Egypt and Marc Anthony a traitor. He was defeated by Octavian at the Battle of Actium and with **Cleopatra** fled to Egypt where they killed themselves.

[49]**Hussars** - The 11th Hussars was a cavalry regiment of the British Army established in 1715. It saw service for three centuries, including the First World War and the Second World War, but then amalgamated with the 10th Royal Hussars [Prince of Wales' Own] to form the Royal Hussars in 1969. During the Second World War, it was deployed in Libya. The Regiment fought the Second Battle of El Alamein in October 1942 and took part in the Allied Invasion of Italy in September 1943.

[50]**The First Battle of El Alamein** [1-27 July 1942] was fought in the Western Desert between Axis Forces [Germany and Italy] of the Panzer Army Africa [Afrika Corps] commanded by Field Marshal Erwin Rommel [the Desert Fox] and Allied [British Imperial] Forces [Britain, British India, Australia, South Africa and New Zealand] of the Eighth Army commanded by General Claude Auchinleck..

The Second Battle of El Alamein [23 October-11 November 1942] took place near the Egyptian railway of El Alamein.

[51]**Montgomery** - Lieutenant General Sir Bernard Law Montgomery took command of the Eighth Army after the death in a plane crash of Lieutenant General William Gott, who had

replaced General Claude Auchinleck.

[52]**Memorial to Victims of Katyn Massacre,** Smolensk, Western Russia.

[53]**The Battle of the Somme** [1 July-18 November 1916] was fought by the Armies of the British [India, Canada, Australia] and French Empires against the German Empire. It was the largest Battle of the First World War on the Western Front. The result was inconclusive and resulted in great loss of life. More than one million men were wounded or killed.

[54]**The French Revolution** [1789-99]**.** Louis XVI was followed by Napoleon as ruler of France. After five failed attempts, European powers finally defeated Napoleon in the Sixth Coalition. The First Empire came to an end in 1814 and the monarchy was restored with the brothers of Louis XVI until the popular uprisings of the July Revolution of 1830. In the spring of 1815, Napoleon came back [the Hundred Days] and the Bourbons flew France but returned to power in July, after his defeat, as a constitutional monarchy. The Roman Catholic Church was re-established as a major power in French politics.

[55]**Charles I** r. from March 1625 to 30 January 1649, when he was executed for high treason. The monarchy was abolished and a republic, called the Commonwealth of England took its place [Oliver Cromwell]. The monarchy was restored to Charles's son, Charles II, in 1660.

[56]**Samurai** were the military nobility and warrior caste of ancient and early-modern Japan. They were usually associated with a clan and with a lord, were trained in military tactics, and followed strict rules.

[57]**Shoguns** were hereditary military dictators in Japan from 1185 to 1868 [with exceptions] and ruled the country, although they were officially appointed by the Emperor.

[58]**Valley of the Queens**- where the wives of the Pharaohs were

buried.

[59]**Hatshepsut**-'Foremost of Noble Ladies' [c.1507-1458 BC] was the fifth Pharaoh of the 18th Dynasty of Egypt, the second historically confirmed female pharaoh and one of the most successful pharaohs.

[60]**French Revolution** [1789-99] Background

Louis XVI, the second of seven children of Louis-the Dauphin of France, died in 1765 and was succeeded by his father Louis XV. At fifteen, he married his cousin, once removed, the 14-year-old Habsburg Archduchess Maria Antonia, Marie Antoinette, youngest daughter of the Holy Roman Emperor Francis I and the Empress Maria Theresa. When his grandfather Louis XV died in 1774, the 19-year-old Dauphin became king and inherited a government deeply in debt and growing unpopularity for the monarchy, as its attempts to reform France in line with the ideals of the Enlightenment were opposed by the nobility. The deregulation of the grain market, advocated by the liberal minister Turgot, resulted in an increase in bread prices which in times of scarcity would lead to mass revolt. National debt increased as a result of Louis' support for North American colonists' independence from Britain, which was sealed by the Treaty of Paris in 1783. The ensuing financial crisis culminated with the Estates General of 1789. There was a growing opposition to the French aristocracy and to the absolute monarchy as represented by Louis and his wife Marie Antoinette. The storming of the Bastille in Paris in 1789 marked the beginning of the French Revolution [to 1799].

The position of the royal family quickly deteriorated. Their flight to Varennes in June 1791 seemed to justify rumours of a political salvation through foreign invasion. But they were quickly caught. Louis XVI was suspended. In 1792 he was arrested and later tried by a tribunal created for the occasion, the National Convention. He was found guilty of high treason and, with his wife Marie Antoinette, was guillotined on 21 January

1793. A 'River of Blood' followed his death as thousands and thousands of people were sent to the block, or summarily executed in the Reign of Terror [5 September 1793-28 July 1794] and finally resulted in the re-establishment of the monarchy, no longer with a king, but an Emperor, Napoleon.

[61]**Patriarch** - the Head of the Orthodox Church in Greece.

[62]**The Battle of Little Bighorn** [June 25-26,1876] in eastern Montana Territory was an overwhelming victory for the Lakota, North Cheyenne and Arapaho, led by several major war leaders including Crazy Horse and Chief Gall inspired by the visions of Sitting Bull. The U.S. 7th Cavalry, including the Custer Battalion led by George Armstrong Custer suffered a major defeat. Five of the 7th Cavalry's twelve companies were annihilated. Custer was killed, as were two of his brothers, a nephew and a brother-in-law.

[63]**Queen Victoria** [1819-1901] of the United Kingdom and Ireland, married Prince Albert of Saxe-Coburg and Gotha [1819-1861]. They had nine children.

[64]**Princess Alice** [1843-1878] was the third child and second daughter of Queen Victoria and Albert, Prince Consort. Of all Victoria's children, she was the first and only one to die at a young age. Princess Alice was the mother of Alexandra of Russia, consort of **Tsar Nicholas II.**

[65]**James Butler Wild Bill" Hickok** was born and raised on a farm in Frontier in Northern Illinois in 1837. He was a folk hero of the American Old West, a man of many and varied skills, and a legendary gunfighter, involved in several shootouts. Among other things, he fought and spied for the Union Army during the American Civil War. He was U.S. Marshal in Kansas. In 1876, Hickok was shot in the back and killed while playing poker in a saloon in Deadwood, South Dakota, by an unsuccessful gambler, Jack McCall. The cards he held in his hand when he was shot [including the ace of spades, the ace of clubs, eight of spades,

and eight of clubs] are known as the 'dead man's hand'. He was 39 years old.

[66]**George V** [1865-1936], second son of Albert Edward, Prince of Wales [later King Edward VII] and grandson of Queen Victoria.

[67]**Prince Albert** of Saxe-Coburg and Gotha [26 August 1819, Coburg, Germany-14 December 1861, Windsor] husband of Queen Victoria.

[68]**Black carriage.** Black became the symbol of Victoria's grief.

[69]**Alice Maud Mary** was the third child and the second daughter of Queen Victoria and Prince Albert. She was born in 1843 and was eighteen-years old when her father died. Alice was the first of Queen Victoria's children, and the only one to die aged 35 in 1878. Her sisters enjoyed long lives.

[70]**Charlotte Bronte** [1816-1855, age 39] was an English novelist and poet, the eldest of the Bronte sister who survived into adulthood and whose novels have become classics of English literature. She published her works under the name of Currer Bell.

[71] **Padre Pio, a**lso known as Saint Pio of Pietralcina**,** Italy, a friar, priest, stigmatist, and mystic, a Saint of the Catholic Church. [1887-1968]

Saint Rita of Cascia [1381-1457] an Italian widow and Augustinian nun canonized in May 1900 by Pope Leo XIII. She is often depicted with roses, because when she was dying, she asked for a rose and, despite being January, one was miraculously found in her garden.

[72]**Richard the Lion Heart [King Richard I]** was the third son of Henry II. He became King of England in 1189, but was based in his Duchy in Aquitaine, inherited from his mother Eleanor. He spent only six months in England and spoke only French. Richard was a Christian commander in the Third Crusade

against Saladin, although he failed to retake Jerusalem from him.

[73]**Akhetaten [Amarna]**-'Horizon of the Aten'-was built by Akhenaten-late 18th Dynasty [c. 1543-1292 BC] in Upper Egypt in around 1346 BC and was situated 312 km south of modern Cairo. It was abandoned shortly after Akhenaten's death [1332 BC]

[74]**Akhenaten-**'Living spirit of the Aten'- believed in one God [the Aten] and introduced fundamental changes in traditional Egyptian religion which did not survive his death. He was a mystic and a visionary and took the role of the Pharaoh to new heights.

[75]**Horemheb**-'Horus is in jubilation' [r.1333-1305 BC*] the last pharaoh of the 18th Dynasty, was not of royal blood, and was the Commander in Chief of the Army. [*Ancient Egypt: A Social History, Cambridge University Press, p184].

[76]**Amun** was the most important god worshipped by Ancient Egyptians and the main seat of his worship was Karnak in Upper Egypt, The Temple was closed by Akhenaten as worship of the new God, the Aten, briefly replaced Amun. The latter's status was reinstated after Akhenaten's death.

[77]**Ay** was the penultimate Pharaoh of the 18th Egyptian Dynasty and a close advisor of two and perhaps three of the pharaohs who reigned before him. He succeeded Tutankhamun after his death, and had a short reign from 1337 to 1333* BC [*Ancient Egypt: A Social History, Cambridge University Press, p184]

[78]In the **Battle of the Teutoburg Fores**t Allied Germanic Tribes ambushed and destroyed three Roman Legions and their auxiliaries, led by Publius Quinctilius Varus [46 BC-Sept.9 AD near Kalkriese, Germany] a Roman General and politician under the first Roman Emperor Augustus, related to the Imperial family. The Germanic tribes were led by Arminius, formerly a Germanic officer of Varus's auxiliaries and a hostage in Rome where he received a military education and Roman citizenship.

He became a trusted advisor to Varus, whom he betrayed by secretly uniting disorganized tribes and forging an alliance with them. He fabricated rumours of a local rebellion and Varus acted immediately. Tragically, he took a detour through territory unfamiliar to Romans, led by Arminius through a route which would facilitate an ambush. Arminius was later assassinated on the orders of rival Germanic chiefs. Rather than be captured, Varus is reported to have killed himself, followed by many of his high- ranking officers, but I did not see this.

[79] **Wilfred Owen** [1893-1918], was an English Poet and Soldier, one of the leading, and most admired, Poets of the First World War. Among his best-known works, most of which were published posthumously, are 'Dulce et Decorum est'; 'Insensibility', 'Futility', and 'Strange Meeting'. His war poetry on the horrors of trenches and as warfare was an indictment of the public perception of war at the time and the absurdly confident patriotic verse written by earlier war poets. Wilfred Owen died on 4 November 1918 aged 25 during the crossing of the Canal exactly one week [almost to the hour] before the signing of the Armistice which ended the war. His mother received the telegram of his death on Armistice Day, while the church bells were ringing in celebration. He is buried at Ors Communal Cemetery.

[80] **Second Battle of the Sambre 4 November 1918.** The Sambre-Oise Canal in Northern France, where Wilfred Owen was shot and died that day. It is only suited for small boats. This site saw one of the last Allied victories of WWI, before the Armistice with Germany which came into effect at 11.00 am on 11 November 1918.

[81] **Craiglockhart Hydropathic** in Edinburgh, was an officers' hospital in WWI, where Wilfred Owen was sent for treatment, together with other soldiers who suffered from shell-shock or neurasthenia on the Western Front. There he met Siegfried Sassoon who was to transform his life. Like many others,

Wilfred Owen was strongly influenced to join the fight by mainstream war propaganda, which he bitterly resented when he saw the reality of war and his soldiers dying around him.

[82] **The white cornette of the Daughters of Charity,** although they do not seem to have served at Craiglockhart, they are what I saw when I woke up and first opened my eyes. These nuns very often appeared to me in meditation and also unexpectedly during the day. They even travelled with me on holidays, when I could see them next to me on empty flight seats and even in my hotel room. WWI Soldiers also did this. At the time, I did not know who they were, nor why they came to me, but their Presence was of great comfort to me.

[83] **Tutankhamun**-'Living Image of the Aten'-was an Egyptian pharaoh of the 18th Dynasty [r.1347-1337BC*] during the New Kingdom. His tomb was discovered intact by Howard Carter in 1922 and he became the most famous of pharaohs, a symbol of Egypt itself. [*Ancient Egypt: A Social History, Cambridge University Press, p.184]

[84] **The Valley of the Kings** stands on the west bank of the Nile, opposite Thebes [Luxor] and was the main place where major royals and privileged nobles were buried during the New Kingdom, over a period of nearly 500 years, from 1050 to 1069 BC.

[85] The entrance room in Tutankhamun's tomb.

[86] **Ankhesenamun-**'Her Life is of Amun'- the third of six known daughters of the Egyptian Pharaoh Akhenaten, half-sister and wife of Tutankhamun.

[87] **Horemheb** [r.1333-1305 BC*] Commander in Chief of the Egyptian Army and the last pharaoh of the 18th Dynasty. He made his vizier Paramesse his successor, who became Ramesses I. [*Ancient Egypt: A Social History, Cambridge University Press]

[88]**Sitting Bull** was a Hunkpapa Lakota holy man and healer [hence his often wearing a headdress with bull's horns] who led his people during years of resistance to US government policies. He was killed by Indian agency police on the Standing Rock Indian Reservation during an attempt to arrest him, at a time when authorities feared he would join the Ghost Dance Movement. [December 15, 1890, aged 58-59] Before the Battle of Little Bighorn he had a vision and saw many soldiers falling upside down in the Lakota camp. About three weeks later, the Confederate Lakota tribes with the Northern Cheyenne defeated and annihilated the 7th Cavalry under Lt. Col. George Armstrong Custer on June 25, 1876.

[89]**The Black Hills,** so called because of their fir trees which look black from the distance, are a small mountain range rising from the Great Plains of North America in western South Dakota and extending into Wyoming, United States. They are sacred and central to Lakota culture. When gold was discovered there in 1874, as a result of Custer's Expedition, miners swept into the Black Hills in a gold rush and more clashes with US government policies.

[90]**Khufu** was the 2nd Pharaoh of the 4th Dynasty which lasted from c. 2613 to 2494 BC, the 'Golden Age' of the Old Kingdom, a time of peace, prosperity, pyramid building at Giza, and foreign trade. The capital was Memphis. The Pharaohs of the 4th Dynasty build in stone, rather than mudbrick. Khufu built the Great Pyramid, one of the Seven Wonders of the World.

[91]**Karnak Templ**e is a huge complex in Egypt. It was built over a long period of time and many pharaohs contributed to the building.

[92]**Sekhmet**-a goddess half lion half woman. She protected the Pharaohs and led them in warfare.

[93]**Thoth-** a god with the body of a man and the head of an ibis and was connected with artistic, religious, scientific creation and

magic, the author of every branch of knowledge, human and divine.

[94] **Temple of Deir el-Bahri**- mortuary temples and tombs on the west bank of the Nile, opposite Luxor in Egypt. The focal point of the Deir el-Bahri complex is the Djeser-Djeseru -'The Holy of Holies'-the Mortuary Temple of Hatshepsut, built by her royal steward and architect [and perhaps lover] Senenmut.

[95] **Hatshepsut-**'Foremost of Noble Ladies'-[1507-1458 BC] 5th pharaoh of the 18th Dynasty and second female pharaoh, the first being Sobekneferu, last ruler of the 12th Dynasty [1806-1802 BC]. Hatshepsut ruled for nearly twenty-two years as pharaoh and was one of the most prolific builders in ancient Egypt. It is not known how she died.

[96] **Charles II** [1661-1700] the son of **Philip IV** and his second wife, and cousin, Mariana of Austria. He was the last ruler of the senior Spanish branch of the House of Habsburg or House of Austria which, after the reign of the Holy Roman Emperor Charles V [1500-1558] had split between its Austrian and Spanish branches. The senior Spanish branch became extinct and was replaced by the House of Bourbon who ruled France and Navarre, Spain, Naples, Sicily, and Parma. The remaining junior Austrian branch became extinct in the male line in 1740 with the death of Holy Roman Emperor Charles VI and completely in 1780 with the death of his eldest daughter Maria Teresa of Austria. It was succeeded by the Vaudemont branch of the House of Lorraine, which styled itself **as** House of Habsburg-Lorraine, although it was often referred to as the House of Habsburg.

[97] **Saxe-Coburg and Gotha** - a Duchy ruled by a branch of the House of Wettin with territories in present-day states of Bavaria and Thuringia in Germany. It lasted from 1826 to 1918. Prince Albert of Saxe-Coburg and Gotha, later Prince Consort, was the husband of Queen Victoria.

[98]**Vice Admiral Horatio Nelson,** 1st Viscount Nelson, 1st Duke of Bronte KB [29 September 1758-21 October 1805]. He was born into a moderately prosperous Norfolk family and joined the navy, rising quickly through the ranks and obtaining his own command in 1778. He suffered illness and unemployment after the American War of Independence, but the French Revolution gave him fresh opportunities and he returned to service. He was wounded several times in combat and lost his right arm.

[99]**Battle of Trafalgar** [21 October 1805] Nelson fought with the Spaniards against Napoleon, aboard HMS Victory, and defeated him. But he was fatally wounded during the battle and died, his body being brought back to England for a state funeral, and became Britain's no. 1 Hero.

[100]There were rumours that **Wilfred Owen** was gay.

[101]**Henrietta Montalba** [1856-14 September 1893] was born in London England, the youngest of four daughters, who all attained considerable success as artists. She was a British sculptor and painter who studied at the Royal College of Art, in South Kensington, with Princess Louise, fourth daughter and sixth child of Queen Victoria. In 1882 Princess Louise painted Henrietta's portrait, which today hangs in the National Gallery of Canada. Montalba then studied at the Accademia delle Belle Arti in Venice. Later she became a pupil of Jules Dalou, the French sculptor, during his residence in London. Henrietta Montalba first exhibited at the Royal Academy in 1876, and also at the Grosvenor Gallery in London, and other galleries. She mainly worked in portraits or fancy busts, some in marble, others in bronze, but the greater part of her work was executed in terracotta [clay]. Her last work was of a more ambitious nature, a life-size figure of 'A Venetian Boy Catching a Crab', in bronze, exhibited at the Royal Academy in 1893 and in Chicago the same year and is in the Victoria and Albert Museum. She was rarely separated from her family, and in her later days resided chiefly at the family home in Venice, Italy. In 1892 her health

began to fail her and after a lingering illness she died in Venice on September 14, 1893, and was buried near her father in the cemetery of San Michele. Henrietta Montalba corresponded with **Robert Browning** and she sculpted his bust in 1883. [Armstrong Browning Library]

[102]**Elizabeth I** [1533-1603] daughter of Henry VIII and Anne Boleyn. She never married. She was the last Tudor monarch.

[103]**The Great Wall of China.** A series of fortifications some of which were built as early as the 7th century BC later joined together, made of stronger materials, to protect Chinese States from nomadic attacks. Especially famous is the wall built 220-206 BC by the 1st Emperor of China, Qin Shi Huang, but little of it remains. Since then, the Great Wall has been rebuilt. The majority ofthe existing wall is from the Ming Dynasty [1368-1644]

The **Mongol Conquest of China** in the 13th Century lasted six decades causing the collapse of the **Jin dynasty** in Western Xia, the **Dali Kingdom,** the **Southern Song,** the **Eastern Xia.** It started with small-scale raids into Western Xia by Genghis Khan [Temujin] in 1205 and 1207. By 1213, Genghis had conquered Jin territory as far south as the Great Wall, while vast numbers of Jin defectors had joined Mongol forces. Genghis died in 1227, but war against the Jin continued under other Khans and ended with their total capitulation in 1234.

[104]**The Khepresh**, the **blue crown or war crown**, worn by New Kingdom pharaohs in battle and in ceremony. It was made of cloth or leather-stained blue covered with a small yellow disc. Like other royal crownsan uraeus was fastened to its front.

[105]In the **Louvre Museum** in Paris [France] there is a delightful painted limestone sculpture of Akhenaten and Nefertiti, dated Year 9, in which they appear young and beautiful, and Akhenaten looks precisely as I saw him in the regression.

[106]**Edward III**, by this time, had acquired a reputation as a

playboy and frequently visited Paris and its brothels. He had many mistresses before and after his marriage of which his wife, Alexandra, was apparently aware. He had illegitimate children whom he never acknowledged.

[107] **Westerbork Transit Camp** during WWII was an assembly point for Jews to be transported to various Nazi Extermination Camps and other Concentration Camps. After the German invasion of the Netherlands, the Camp, which was erected by the Dutch government in 1939 to house Jewish refugees fleeing from Nazi Germany, was turned into a Deportation Camp. Between July 1942 and September 1944 nearly every week a train took its human cargo to Auschwitz-Birkenau, Sobibor, Bergen-Belsen, Theresienstadt. From 1942 to 1945 over one hundred thousand people passed through these Camps, mostly to be killed on arrival. Only five thousand two hundred people survived, mainly in Theresienstadt and Bergen- Belsen, or were liberated at Westerbok by the Allies.

[108] **Anne Frank** [12 June 1929-February/March 1945]-a German born Jew, who went into hiding in Amsterdam in 1942 with her family, to escape Nazi persecution, but they were betrayed in 1944 and taken by the Gestapo [Secret State Police] to Concentration Camps. Anne and her sister Margot were then taken to Auschwitz and then to Bergen- Belsen where they died [probably of typhus] shortly afterwards. While in hiding captivity, Anne wrote a Diary which was published posthumously in 1947. The Diary of Anne Frank has been translated into many languages and inspired plays, documentaries and films. Anne was seen by many as the embodiment of the annihilation of youth during the War.

[109] **Carbine**. The carbine was originally created for the cavalry, but it was adopted by nations around world after WWI because of its versality and lightness of weight.

[110] **American Landings in Normandy** [6 June 1944] and the start of the Battle of Normandy [6 June/29 August 1944], one of

the bloodiest Battles of WWII against strong German entrenchments.

[111]**The Battle of Waterloo** [18 June 1815] in present-day Belgium. Two armies of the Seventh Coalition-a British Allied army under the Duke of Wellington and a Prussian army under the Prince of Wahlstatt-defeated the French army of Emperor Napoleon Bonaparte and marked the end of the Napoleonic Wars.

[112]**Normandy Landings, known as D-Day, 6 June 1944.** The Allied invasion of Normandy in Operation Overlord during WWII, the largest seaborne invasion in history. Over 156,000 troops landed on the beaches in the Battle of Normandy, a day that changed the outcome of the Second World War.

[113]**The Olmecs tribes** were the earliest known major civilizations in Mesoamerica [1500-400 BCE] in south- central Mexico, present-day Veracruz and Tabasco.

[114]**The Battle of Cape Bon.** On 13 December 1941, HMS Sikh with Allied Forces, Legion, Maori, and the Dutch vessel HNLMS Isaac Sweers, sank the Italian cruisers Alberico da Barbiano and Alberto di Giussano.

[115]**Vicky, Victoria, Princess Royal,** eldest daughter of Queen Victoria of the United Kingdom and Prince Albert of Saxe-Coburg and Gotha

[116]The **Inquisition** - a group of institutions within the Catholic Church to fight heresy. It started in 12th century France. The term 'Medieval Inquisition' relates to these courts up to the mid-15th Century. Later, the Inquisition expanded to other European countries, as a result of the Protestant Reformation and the Catholic Counter- Reformation. The institution survived as part of the Roman Curia and in 1965 it became the 'Congregation for the Doctrine of the Faith'.

[117]**Princess Alice** [Alice Maud Mary, 25 April 1843-14 December 1878] Grand Duchess of Hesse and by Rhine from

1877 to 1878, third child and second daughter of Queen Victoria and Prince Albert. She was the first of Queen Victoria's nine children to die. Alice was a devoted patron of women's causes with an interest in nursing, especially in the work of Florence Nightingale. When Hesse became involved in the Austro-Prussian War, Darmstadt [where she resided] filled with wounded soldiers and Alice, heavily pregnant, devoted most of her time to their care and to the management of field hospitals. One of her organisations, the Princess Alice's Women Guild, took over much of the running of the state's military hospitals. Her work, down-to-earth speaking, breast-feeding, and unorthodox manners, upset Queen Victoria so much that eventually they hardly spoke to one another. In 1877, Alice became Grand Duchess upon the accession of her husband, but her health suffered as a result of increased responsibilities. In late 1878, diphtheria infiltrated the Hessian Court. Alice nursed her family for over a month before becoming ill and dying late that year. She was the mother of Tsarina Alexandra Feodorovna of Russia [Wife of Tsar Nicholas II], maternal grandmother of Louis Mountbatten and maternal great- grand mother of Prince Philip, Duke of Edinburgh [consort of Queen Elizabeth II]. Another daughter, Elisabeth, who married Grand Duke Sergei Alexandrovich of Russia was, like the Tsarina and her family, killed by the Bolsheviks in 1918.

[118] **Death of Friedrich**, youngest and favourite son of Princess Alice, on 29 May 1873 after falling 20 feet from a window. He suffered from haemophilia and the internal bleeding could not be stopped. Alice never recovered from his death. In 1875, after the birth of her daughter Marie, she resumed public duties, including fund-raising, medical and social work, and kept in close touch with social reformer Octavia Hill. Meanwhile, relations with her husband deteriorated, due to intellectual disparity between them.

[119] **Craiglockart War Hospital-**Edinburgh**.** During the war, Wilfred Owen had some very traumatic experiences. He fell into a shell hole and suffered concussion; he was blown up by a

trench mortar and spent several days unconscious on an embankment lying amongst the remains of one of his fellow officers. He was found suffering from shell shock or neurasthenia and sent to Craiglockhart War Hospital for treatment. There he met fellow poet Siegfried Sassoon. At Craiglockhart he was happy and made new friends in the artistic and literary circles of Edinburgh and did some teaching at the Tynecastle High School in a poor area of the city. In November he was discharged from Craiglockhart, judged fit for light regimental duties. He spent winter in Scarborough, North Yorkshire, and in March 1918 was sent to the Northern Command Depot at Ripon, where he worked on a number of poems, including 'Futility' and 'Strange Meeting'. He spent his 25th birthday quietly at Ripon Cathedral. Although he might have remained on home-duty indefinitely, he decided to return to active service in France in July 1918, a decision which his friend Siegfried Sassoon violently opposed. At the end of August 1918, Owen returned to the front line and on 1 October 1918, he replaced the commander who had died and stormed a number of enemy strong points near the village of Joncourt with units of the 2nd Manchesters. He was killed in action on 4 November 1918 during the crossing of the Sambre-Oise Canal, exactly one week [almost to the hour] before the signing of the Armistice which ended the war and was promoted to the rank of Lieutenant the day after his death. He was awarded the Military Cross 'For conspicuous gallantry and devotion to duty on the attack on the Fonsomme line on October 1st/2nd, 1918... He personally manipulated a captured enemy machine gun from an isolated position and inflicted considerable losses on the enemy. Throughout he behaved most gallantry.'

[120]**A Wedding like a Funeral.** Princess Alice became engaged to Prince Louis of Hesse, a minor German royal, on 30 April 1861. Although her father Prince Albert died on 14 December 1861, the wedding took place as planned on 1 July 1862, in the dining room of Osborne House, converted into a temporary chapel. Alice wore a simple white dress, and black mourning

clothes before and after the ceremony. Victoria, sitting in an armchair, was shielded from view by the Prince of Wales and Prince Alfred, her second son, who cried throughout the service, while the Queen held back her tears. Victoria later remarked to her eldest daughter Victoria, that the ceremony was 'more of a funeral than a wedding'.

[121]**An intellectual Soulmate:** the theologian David Friedrich Strauss, a controversial figure at the time, who offered Alice an intellectual companionship her husband was unable to provide, and was regularly invited to the New Palace to read to Alice privately.

[122]**John Brown**, served Queen Victoria in Balmoral as an outdoor servant from 1849 to 1861 and as a personal attendant from 1861 [after Prince Albert's death] to 1883. He became a good friend and a companion to the Queen, but the relationship was strongly objected to by family and courtiers, who questioned the nature of their relationship with talks of a wedding, which has not been proved so far.

[123]**'I was not happy, nor unhappy.'** After the death of her son Friedrich ['Frittie'] in 1873, Alice became more attached to her only surviving son, Ernest, and her baby daughter Marie. In 1875, she resumed her public work. Her relation with her husband deteriorated as she felt the deepening gulf between them, her complex nature and his simpler one, lacking intellectual curiosity and depth, but she remained his strong and loyal supporter.

[124]**The First World War** known as The Great War, 'the War to end all Wars' with more than 70 million military personnel, 9 million Soldiers' deaths and 13 million civilians' deaths

[125]**The Second World War-**1 September 1939-German Invasion of Poland-2 September 1945. A global War involving the majority of countries, including all the great powers, and more than 100 million personnel from more than 30 countries,

the deadliest conflict in human history with 70 to 85 million deaths, more civilians than military personnel killed.

[126]**Emperor Hirohito**, was the 124th emperor of Japan [29 April 1901-7 January 1989] ruled the Empire of Japan from 1926 to 1947, after which he was Emperor of the state of Japan until his death.

[127]**Battle of Midway** [4-7 June 1942] was an American victory, a major naval battle in the Pacific Theatre of WWII six months after Japan's attack on Pearl Harbor.

[128]**Charlotte Bronte**, [21 April 1816-31 March 1855] English novelist and poet, the eldest of three sisters who survived into adulthood and whose novels became classics of English literature.

[129]**Chakras**, energy points in the body.

Printed in Great Britain
by Amazon

15675527R00142